Black Sterling

Khadijah

ISBN: 1513625187
ISBN-13: 9781513625188

Connect with the Author. www.blacksterling.uk

www. twitter.com/darkgirlboss

DEDICATION

My Father

My father, the late Edgar Adolphus Baker(1930 - 2015). Handsome warrior, exceptional athlete, and an intelligent, charming & witty gentleman whom I loved and admired. I miss him dearly.

My Mother

My mother, Dorothy nee Ward, who unwittingly gave me drive, determination, strength of character and the will to succeed. Without those traits I would not have survived the numerous downs of my life and had the will and perseverance to succeed.

My Granddaughter

My first grandchild Kiah Hassan, for her insight and valuable opinion on helping me decide the book title and cover. Cynthia Marva Charles My 'one of a kind' Best friend: 25/09/12 RIP

ACKNOWLEDGMENTS

Special Thanks: To Professor Manu Ampim for allowing me to use his research on the stolen legacy of Ancient Egyptian history.

My launch Team: Sami Rafiq; Jackie Baker, Louise Pearce, and Scott Williams thanks for executing the successful launch of Black Sterling, getting it out there for all to read. An extra special thanks to Sami for naming this book. Good call Sam! And thanks to Patricia Farrell for editing.

Most of all I should like to thank Allah the Almighty who helped me write this book as a legacy for my decedents a hundred years from now. Alhamdulillah.

If Law Was Passed Tomorrow Stating:

We are no longer housing black people on our council estates, we are not lending black people money for mortgages, we are not allowing black people to shop in our supermarkets, we are not allowing black people to work on our corporate plantations.

How would you survive?

Find Out What You Need To Do Now! To Escape the Systems of Control and Oppression and operate in an alternative Collective Black Economic System. In this book BLACK STERLING

By UK Author Khadijah Ward
An escapee of the Corporate Plantation

CONTENTS

PREFACE

"Without commerce and industry, a people perish economically. The Negro is perishing because he has no economic system." – Marcus Garvey

Peace Be upon you beautiful people, and thank you for purchasing my book. May you find it an empowering guide for you to achieve unity amongst yourselves, collective wealth, and liberation from the oppressive euro-centric systems that you unfortunately find yourselves in.

Is the black man perishing because he has no economic system? And what is economic self-reliance? I shall explain, but first I would like to illustrate the idea with an example.

Imagine this...

Communities where you are revered not undermined. Communities with no police harassment and brutality, no gang warfare, no systematic jailing or slaying of your young men. Schools for your children that are built and run by you.

Your commerce, housing, workplace, industries and institutions that you rely upon for your livelihood hold your race in high regard. Communities where wealth is created shared and multiplied, and you and yours prosper.

Sounds great right! Well, that place, that dream, is where black people as a nation have power and control the politics of your own people. You function independently of the current mainstream euro-centric systems. The infrastructures that you rely upon are owned by black people, run by black people, for black people.

You are in control of your own lives, your own housing, your own institutions. You are a self-reliant nation with wealth and power within your own communities.

Economic self-reliance, from a black perspective, is total liberation of the black nation, meaning that you should control the economy of your community. The economic infrastructures that you rely upon, are owned and run by black people, for black people. From education systems, housing, industry, corporations and monetary institutions, all independent of the oppressive Eurocentric mainstream infrastructures. Economic self-reliance is power!

Self-reliance of the black man is not a new concept it has been done many times before by your ancestors, pre and post the African Holocaust.

Malcolm X through the Nation of Islam (NoI) transformed communities with the NoI economic blueprint as a guide.

He encouraged African-Americans to build communities that would stand on their own and quit the mainstream, to live clean and disciplined lives, and to obtain dignity through self-reliance.

Not only did he speak about self-reliance and encourage his people. He also took practical steps, and through the unity of his comrades he succeeded in cleaning up black neighbourhoods in the US.

They drove out drug dealers, got rid of liquor stores and developed business and industry for the community.

Another positive of self-reliant systems is your children. If they are living in black wealthy productive communities where they have pride in who they are, and there are prospects for the future, their interactions with police forces would diminish as would the need to hang on street corners, engage in criminal activities and other self-destructive behaviours.

Imagine a positive. You had economic control, you owned industries and had power over yourself within the systems that operate through your own communities and you were not reliant upon the current systems that you live under. Your life would improve considerably and chances of experiencing racism would dramatically decrease if not be eliminated altogether.

INTRODUCTION

"*Black people must do for self or suffer the consequences.*" — Elijah Muhammed

Elijah Muhammed's statement is simple yet powerful. He was basically stating that if you, black people, are not self-reliant, but dependent upon the systems of others you will be subject to an oppressive existence with negative outcomes.

The situation of the black man today is evidence that we as a people are not in control of our own community, neither are we responsible for our economic condition and as a result as a nation you are suffering.

As a nation we do not own property, resources or institutions. We are dependent upon euro-centric infrastructures and systems for all of our basic human needs, to include; housing, education, jobs and financial attainment.

These systems upon which you and I rely, execute oppression, injustice, inequality, indignity, brutality, poverty, and even death for some of you or your loved ones. They oppress you to limit your social organisation, financial success and freedom as a nation.

Since the days of slavery, your life has been controlled through systems by rich and powerful men that do not look like you. You are their commodities, the source for their wealth. Essentially you are modern day slaves.

Your whole life and well-being depends upon these systems. Systems which are structured to mould, control, shape and train the mind and behaviour of you and your children to be dependent upon it.

The consequences of your dependency upon these structures and systems ultimately leaves you demobilised and poor. It is a structure in which you have no place as members of such a Noble race, that is decedents of the African people. In the present day, the greatness, glory and grandeur that is the historic African civilisation, is lost in the minds of black people, through the abomination of what was once the African Holocaust and its legacy.

I am therefore compelled to write this book, as I bear witness to the destruction and the decline of our Noble Nation through purpose-built euro-centric, centenary systems.

And it is my duty, as a member of your noble nation, to help make positive change in the minds and actions of my community in order to steer you towards liberation, collective black wealth and control of self.

This book, Black Sterling, not only deciphers institutionalised, systemic racism and oppressive economic systems, but it also proposes solutions to escape from them.

It will guide you towards the blueprint, the proven path of collective wealth that your people before you have taken to enable power and control of their own existence.

There are seven inspirational and practical action steps that you can implement after reading this book to start working towards a life, where you, and your brothers and sisters share the fruits of what the power of unity and liberation brings, economic wealth and control of self. Prepare yourself to operate in an alternative system… a Black Economic System.

In this introduction, I have given you a picture of inspiration on using imagination to attain reality as a start, and we will get back to that. For now you really need to step out and take a look at the nasty reality of your systemic oppression, and only when you see it for what it really is will you take the necessary steps required to escape it.

Fasten your seat belts people, here we go…

BLACK 'A DIRTY WORD'

Black people of the world are feared, hated, envied and oppressed due to their skin colour and what that colour represents... Greatness!
— Khadijah Ward

You're probably wondering why this section is entitled 'Black a dirty word,' right.

Well, before I tell you that, it's important for you to understand that in order to escape the impact of systemic racism and achieve collective power and control of self, you must first fully understand how the system operates and controls you.

How each tiny component fits together to give a complete system, and how that system makes you, as a black person in western society, behave and feel about yourself, and also makes others behave towards you.

During and post slavery, negative images of black people have been created and spread to the minds of the masses through communication channels, institutions and in the family home. Black continues to be portrayed as something to fear and perceived as bad.

Systemic racism is explained throughout this book, not so that you can act as a victim and shout empty chants of racism, or be angry and anti-white people, those actions are a complete waste of time and energy, and serve no positive outcomes.

We are not anti-white, we are pro-black and the explanations are given in order that you may have the facts presented before you, in that you are crystal clear regarding the power of the system, its grasp upon you and its lethal negative impact upon your whole life.

Once you have the facts and you are able to see exactly how you are controlled, only then will you be able to take the necessary steps of combined consciousness and action towards your independence from the system.

Actions that will liberate you from the impact of systemic oppression and bring for you and your nation, self-reliance, collective wealth and economic leadership.

The introduction name 'black a dirty word' is not meant in a literal sense, it is my play on words to demonstrate that it is understood that black is perceived as negative in the eyes of the western world, I know the game and I am not afraid to talk about it.

Some people may believe that we shouldn't get tied up in the meaning of words relating to black, they are just words after all, 'sticks and stones...' right. Wrong! It is important to understand the rationale and power of words, particularly when they are being used for mind control tools to create stereotypes, reinforce negative messages and control behaviour.

HIP-HOP - A State of Hypnosis

The power of words and how they can influence behaviour is a matter which is not usually addressed or analysed. However we should be aware that words can be used as a movement of inspiration or can have catastrophic consequences when used incorrectly particularly when combined with music.

Music is the most powerful medium in the world. It can be used to spread any message that one likes to influence the masses.

Music generates feelings, when we create music, hear or play it we feel good, and it can be inspiring, mesmerising and influence our behaviour.

We see the power of words-lyrics in the music industry today and the impact that it has upon the youth, particularly the genre of hip-hop, and the rappers of this world are in a sense unproclaimed leaders for the black youth.

They have the power to influence and mould our young people with their lyrics through hip-hop.

Hip-hop, an example of the forever evolving and change of music with its tremendous influence has been around for a long time, but it really picked up its pace in the early 1980s-1990s giving us artists who rapped conscious lyrics, such as Grandmaster Flash with The Message, that showed the negative outcomes of integration of the system.

KRS-One - Sound of da Police is just one of his conscious rap tunes; Public Enemy - fight the power. The NWA's 'fuck the police' saw violence against the US police forces rise up to 300%.

Now that is influence! To be able dictate behaviour in such a way through lyrics. That is not to say that I condone violence, it is an example of the powerful influence of music and hip hop lyrics that can control behaviour.

The 1990s also gave us, the beautiful and highly intelligent Tupac Shakur, who also spoke consciously outside of his music.

Run DMC sang 'My Adidas' in the 1990s and Adidas sneaker sales sky rocketed.

In 2016 hundreds of people were seen queuing for days to purchase limited edition Adidas trainers designed by rapper Kanye west in collaboration with Adidas. Now that's power and influence.

Some rappers have recorded tunes for alcohol brands including Malt liquor; Courvoisier, which boosted the brands sales by 30%. Cristal

Champagne; Vodka - Ciroc's sales reportedly sky rocketed by 70% after a particular artist became its brand ambassador.

Myx Fusions Moscato's monthly wine sales have reportedly surged a whooping 500% since an artists part-ownership and endorsement of the drink.

Music, rap music in particular is a powerful and influential tool over the black youth, and artists are fully aware of their influence.

Rappers have the power to make the people conscious of their situation, they could start a black revolution through their music, but they choose not to. Instead they act irresponsibly and selfishly towards their people.

Black celebrities receive millions of dollars, and they refuse to say anything about the plight of black people, or do anything to change our situation as they work within, and for the system.

Without caring about the consequences of their actions, they influence young people to a hypnotic state to aspire to nothing. Through the glamorisation of thug life, drugs, guns, drinking alcohol, buying the next brand of trainers as a goal, individual excessive wealth, jewellery, and above all the denigration of the black woman.

There is nothing wrong with the general idea of wealth or striving to be wealthy, but there is everything wrong with it when it is obtained at the cost of black lives, destroying the minds of, and killing the young and impressionable black man.

Many rap artists of today are slaves to the music industry, white corporations get richer and more powerful as black people collaborate with them in the destruction of black youth which is the pinnacle of irresponsible slave mentality.

The systems design encourages slave mentality behaviour as that type of behaviour enables the systems principles to flourish.

Further on in the book we discuss slave mentality in more depth, and in 'My Story is Your Story' section we discuss agents of the system that execute the interests and principles of the system and shut you down if you don't abide by the rules.

As a taster we will discuss the Grime artist Bashy's underground smash hit video 'Black Boys' 2007 which was banned from UK television by TV regulators Ofcom, who claimed that the song is considered to be 'racist.' Are you kidding me with that statement?

Claiming that the song is racist is an act of reverse psychology, an issue that we will discuss in chapter one, 'Who Controls the System that Controls You.'

The rap video was shot in celebration of Black History Month, and was inspiring, highlighting the positives of black males. It had been shown on MTV Base and Channel U.

It is clear why it has been deemed racist. The reason being is that the system does not want black males to feel good about themselves to be inspired to do good, therefore they destroy any attempts that may achieve that.

The controllers of the system realise that youths can be reached and their behaviour controlled through music. That is the reason you have seen the change in the hip-hop industry over the years, from conscious to hypnosis.

Most of the artists play along because their end goal is to obtain wealth through the system. It is evident that they clearly only care about themselves and are aiding and abetting the destruction of the black youth.

Black Sheep of the family: Again we see how words are used to denigrated the black man, through every day usage what is deemed to be normal.

If I asked you right now to give me a list of popular phrases used nationally that show the colour black in a positive light, I bet you could not think of even one.

You may however, be aware of some of the matters that are associated with black as every day references and terms as acceptable normalities that suggest that Black is bad. Such as Black sheep, which implies one is the bad one of that family or group.

Black Wednesday: Represents a bad day for British politics and economics. 16 September 1992, when the British Conservative government was forced to withdraw the pound sterling from the European Exchange Rate Mechanism (ERM) after it was unable to keep the pound above its agreed lower limit in the ERM.

The Plague: 'Black Death': As it is known, resulted in the deaths of an estimated 75 to 200 million people and peaking in Europe in the years 1346–53. It killed 30–60% of Europe's total white population.

Blacklisted, Black Market, Black magic, Black mail, Black-Balled, are more of the negative connotations associated with the word black.

Death itself is associated with the colour black, and the list goes on. These are all reminders of when something bad happened or that is simply bad in itself, and the term black is the overall reminder of bad occurrences and events.

Psychological Warfare

We have established the words have the potential to produce positive or negative consequences, both in thought and in the actions of people behaviour.

Just think about the associations of the word black, that we have discussed, from the perspective of a child, black or white. When that child hears those associations day after day, year after year throughout its life it is very easy to see black as something that is bad.

In opposition to that, white is portrayed and associated with all that is good and pure. Even the one they call 'Jesus' is portrayed as white, and that is about as pure as it gets, as the West believe, and would have the rest of the world believe that 'Jesus' is the son of God, and that image is portrayed as white.

So being white you are in the image of God. And to see that symbol portrayed in any other way for them would be deemed blasphemous. As a white member of a Church once said it was blasphemous to suggest that the one they call 'Jesus' was black.

This portrayal of a white 'Jesus' suggests that if you are the same colour of the one they call God's son then surely you must be superior to all of those not of that colour.

In comparison to how the colour black is portrayed to that of white, 'godly' you can see how white children will grow up feeling very good about their colour, and black children will not.

These are simply psychological warfare tricks that you and I are subject to beginning during the African Holocaust.

These small psychological tricks viewed in isolation may not seem much to worry, or even think about, however they are in fact part of a larger system, and when analysed in conjunction with that system you will see just how deadly they really are.

Black Fear and the Gun

We have discussed negative associations with the colour black which brings us to 'black fear' that is white people's fear of the black man.

White people are actually in charge of the system, and indeed the free world. They are all powerful and control everything to include you and I. So if they have the power what reason would they have to fear him, the black man?

The answer is the fear is manufactured, and in their minds there is good reason for it which is this:

The power and control that is currently in the hands of the white controllers of the system, was taken by force with the gun, and during the process of taking the power, they bestowed upon the black man unimaginable atrocities.

Therefore the fear is real, it is fear of the black man's retaliation that he may regain his power. And one of the methodologies to ensure that the black man does not retaliate to regain his power, is to spread the fear of him throughout the white population to create an offence system.

The distorted psychological image portrayed of the black man is that he is big, bad and ugly, with animal-like aggression, cunning, untrustworthy with the ability to kill. Therefore you, if white must be on-guard to keep him in his place and protect yourself.

The pathological fear of the black man is synonymous with the fear of the lion. For example if you found yourself in the jungle and you came across a lion, you would be afraid, because you have been taught that lions are something to be feared.

Therefore you would arm yourself to pacify the lion, minimise or eliminate the potential threat of said lion, and if you had a gun you would use it. Right!

This paranoid fear of the black man is the same. It provides white people with the justification of an offence system to protect themselves by any means necessary, and in-turn it justifies the atrocious treatment of the black man, in ensuring your threat of retaliation is minimised with the proactive measures of keeping you under control, submissive and at the bottom of the world's ladder.

Ultimately the current rich and powerful stay rich and powerful and you, black people remain as their human resource and commodity.

Power of the Trigger

Black fear is permeated from the highest levels in society. Legislation, law and order is one of the mechanical cogs used in the wheel of black fear and oppression.

If the State enacts legislation, and executes that legislation through the guise of law and order, it appears as if there is no wrong doing on the part of the executer of the law, right.

Even though in the twenty-first century African-Americans have the right to bear arms, it has done them no good. And the world has seen how the police exercise their legal powers using the gun, again protecting themselves from fear of the 'dreaded black man'.

Even African-Americans with licences to carry guns have been shot and killed where they stand by police. In fact, countless African-Americans, man, woman and child have fallen under police brutality and their cold-blooded murdering ways.

And with every murder, the police hide behind 'I was in fear of my life' and their right to 'shoot to kill,' that's because 'black fear' is enshrined in the minds of law makers thus providing a legal pathway for police to execute the myth of black fear.

We should remember our brothers and sisters across the water in the US whom have also had their life taken by use of the gun as the US law enforcement are allowed to carry guns as an everyday part of their duties to kill with impunity.

The death of black people at the hands of law enforcement is tragic. Black people are treated like animals, and terminated like vermin as the system hides behind their laws in the protection of their own.

Here are just a few of our US brothers and sisters that were taken by a system that is designed to kill us.

Emitt Till, Tamera Rice, Laquin MacDonald, Freddie Gray, Jason Harrison and Philander Castile who's tragic murder was live streamed by his girlfriend on Facebook. The live stream didn't help get justice for Philander as the filthy pig murdering cop was found not guilty as he declared his defence as being 'in fear of his life.'

This same credulous acceptance of the narrative of fear is why Officer Betty Jo Shelby was acquitted in the killing of Terence Crutcher; why a grand jury declined to charge Officer Timothy Loehmann in the killing of Tamir Rice, a 12-year-old; and why a jury deadlocked in the case of Michael Slager, a South Carolina police officer who shot and killed Walter Scott during a traffic stop. They all cited fear of their life. And with a black victim that is all it takes to avoid any punishment for taking a black life.

All you have to do is open your eyes and see that the disease of 'Black fear' accompanied by the Licence to kill is systemic across the United States, United Kingdom and Europe.

Remember, throughout our everyday lives the word 'black' is purposely associated with negative connotations and all that is bad. In an attempt to create a psychological colour image complex to demonise the black man and sustain white supremacy.

It works in conjunction with a larger system that reinforces subconscious messages that enact particular behaviours that we talk more about in chapter one.

The Most Powerful Colour in Existence

We have spoken about black as a 'dirty word' and black fear, now let us look at black from a positive angle, as a starting point of uplifting your consciousness.

It is more than necessary to counter-act the stigma and associations with the colour black, as it is obvious that black is portrayed as bad as part of the psychological tricks to make others loathe you and for you to loathe yourselves. After all you were not the ones who created the terms.

Why I say it is obvious is that, the truth of the matter is, black is not bad, in fact black, is actually the most powerful colour in existence.

As a colour, black has the ability to attract to it all rays of colour and light. It is an absorber of both light and cosmic radiation; Black cap-stones were often placed on Egyptian pyramids and obelisks due to the powers inherent in its colour.

Solar energy cells are black; Dry cell batteries are powered by black chemicals. Energy is drawn towards black substances where it can be stored for a determined period of time and used as needed.

Then of course you have black human beings and all of your powerful and unique attributes. (See below, Beautifully Unique.)

Black, in essence has always been, and shall always be, a source of power and influence. That is the real reason that black people of the world are feared, hated, envied and oppressed... their skin colour and what that skin colour essentially represents... Greatness! I'm quoting myself.

Beautifully Unique - Time to big up black people!

The African people are the most beautiful and unique people to have graced the earth. I can honestly say that I get a buzz from being black, it feels great!

As a people we are peaceful and have a natural love of humanity. The beauty and uniqueness is evident in our physical make-up like no other, genetic talents and genius in creation. It is such a powerful gene that even when it is mixed with any other race it is still the most dominant gene.

The black man's hair type is unique to his race only, different from that of any other race. All the other races have natural straight hair, and cannot possess or even synthetically recreate your hair type without mixing genetically with you.

The natural talents and abilities of black people are unprecedented. Natural rhythm, athletic ability, dancing ability, and musical genius, again all unique to the black race, without any training, for which you should be proud. You are second to none.

A Work of Art

Sculptured features; Natural athletic physique, defined and muscular; beautiful dark smooth and shiny skin; full luscious sensual lips and full rounded tight buttocks. Can only be described as a work of natural art and sculpture.

No other race has your attributes without having genetically mixed with the black race, or had them artificially implanted.

Other races know that these attributes are beautiful, and they long for what you have. They won't tell you directly to your face, but the evidence speaks for itself.

And instead of being revered, in particular the black woman, you are ridiculed and made fun of for what she has naturally, and your god-given natural attributes are things stolen from you credited to other races.

For instance, we hear full lips being referred to as 'the Paris lip,' when I have vivid memories of being called 'rubber lips' as an insult. Corn row as the 'french plait' Braids as 'the Bo Derek.' African buttocks as 'the JLO butt'

The black woman's buttocks used to be something to be mocked and pointed at starting with Saartjie Baartman, whose buttocks and enlarged labia had thrilled and scandalised Georgian London in 1810 where she was put on display in what can only be described as a human zoo.

Now however, the black woman's buttocks has become the height of want and fashion, as women both celebrity and ordinary non-black women alike beg surgeons for butt implant paddings and injection of fat into behinds for full and rounded buttocks to mimic the black woman.

The subject rarely comes up but let's be honest The frequent use of sun beds is at least one indication that people that use them want darker skin.

Sun beds make you darker, so the logical conclusion is that if you sit under a sun bed, you want to be darker.

Then there is the matter of people with naturally thin lips injecting chemical fillers for full lips.

All of the above are evidences of wanting to imitate the black woman's attributes.

Black people develop trends that people follow. For instance the African movement that requires an African sculptured backside to execute the move correctly is now being referred to as 'twerking'. Miley Cyrus and others that lack the appropriate rear... please stop it. It looks ridiculous.

You are naturally athletic looking and in your abilities. It is just one of the many talents that can be uniquely associated to you.

Dancing, for black people is as natural as breathing, you have since the beginning of time, it is in your genes, and it is your culture.

Do you know any black person that does not have natural dance rhythm? All the famous artists known for their dance moves are black and the dance moves that they create are obviously African influence, it remains in your genes.

Music! You don't just have contributions to the music industry, you are the music industry, and without black people it would not exist. That is all genres, including Opera and Classical music.

Singing: When you sing, truly it sends shivers down the spine, the feeling that you give to others through song is simply amazing. During slavery times the slave owners were astonished that everyone could sing. Something which fortunately they could not physically take away.

I once heard Whitney Houston singing soprano. Oh My God! It sent shivers down my spine. She was not trained how to sing opera, like most professional opera singers. It was natural.

The music industry is what it is today, because of the feelings that you give to people when you execute your God given talents.

White people understand this, and they understand that music creates feelings of a high and that generates money. Every body wants to feel good, and music will do that to you.

That is the reason you find the economics of the music industry is managed behind the scenes by rich white men.

Love Your Unique Qualities

Recognise your beauty and love yourself and in turn love your brothers and sisters.

Be proud that black is beautifully unique, believe that you are beautiful because you are.

Believe in yourself as a black person. Say it again and again to yourself. Black is beautiful! You are a vibrant and unique race, embrace your uniqueness, love yourself and each other. It may sound gushy but I mean it. Say and believe it, it will give you confidence and self-esteem.

Black Sterling Action Step 1

Remember, the main issues that we discussed in this section, will help you implement the action step.

The action steps throughout this book are necessary to help you escape the oppressive system and prepare you with a competitive advantage to operate in an alternative black economic system of collective black wealth, self-reliance and governance.

Don't be afraid when you hear the terms economic self-reliance, collective black wealth and control of self, or black economic system. That fear you may feel, or any resistance to change is just the work of the systems oppression playing tricks with your mind.

It is so sophisticated in the way that it messes with your mind to make you afraid of the consequences of not being integrated within the system even though you are oppressed and under its control.

The introduction asked you to imagine what your life would be like if black people had collective wealth, political and financial influence and control of self.

The second part showed you how your skin colour is used as a negative tool to divide you. And the third part was all about your positive attributes to make you recognise and appreciate your unique beauty.

So, your first action step is two-fold but simple:

1a. Imagine and so it shall be. The imagination is a powerful tool, and before reality can be created it must first be imagined. If you do not imagine it, obtaining it would be virtually impossible.

You know, every book, every movie, every business, started with a dream and steps were taken thereafter to make the dream a reality.

Before I became a published author I imagined it, I could see it, I then took steps to realise the dream. So, the first part of the action is to use your imagination and create your reality by imagining the outcome.

Every spare minute of everyday, plant the picture in your subconscious mind of what your community and life would look like if your people were united in collective economic power and control of self.

Once you continue to plant the picture you will take the natural steps required to contribute towards making the dream a reality.

Those steps may include associating more with people who are already on a path to unity and collective organising. Or, seeking out black-owned businesses to purchase from as a priority, or contributing your skills and knowledge to help form the economic future. Or even donating funds.

1b. <u>Form alliances and unify with people of the same skin colour</u>. You all have one common denominator, and that is your skin colour, which determines how the system and others in society treats you.

We spoke of this at length. Even though your colour is used as a tool to degrade you, you must now flip the script and own it! Your skin colour must now be the very thing that unites you with others like you.

Forget about what makes you different from other black people, like geography for instance, or background, beliefs or financial status. Or whether you are Christian, Muslim, Atheist or Buddhist.

Society does not care that you are a Jamaican Christian, or that you are a Trinidadian Muslim. You are all seen as black, and treated in accordance with what black skin represents in the eyes of the controllers of the system.

Therefore, that common denominator of skin colour that you share with others of different religions and Islands or countries around the world, must be the very thing that acts as your alliance and unity. Your black skin is your power use it to work in unity.

Who controls the system that controls you, read on...

CHAPTER ONE

WHO CONTROLS THE SYSTEM THAT CONTROLS YOU?

"*The system is for you or against you there is no middle ground.*"—Kwame Ture

Remember in the introduction we looked at one aspect of the system relating to the colour black. Now you must look with more depth to see inside of the deadly system that we all crave to be a part of before you can escape it.

Tell me, who do you think controls and governs the housing corporations that your brothers and sisters rely upon for their most basic of human needs?

Who controls the education institutions where your children are taught about white history and white heroes? Where they are racial abused by teachers; are four times more likely to receive permanent exclusion from school than any other racial group?

Who controls the industries where you are nine times more likely to be refused work, and discriminated against in employment due to your race?

Who controls the media that demonises the black man with propaganda fuelling hysteria of the alleged "inherent" nature of black criminality and lawlessness?

Who governs the policing of you and your children to the point where they are harassed, disproportionately stopped & searched, arrested, brutalised, and slayed!

The answer is... The controller of the system, the rich and powerful white Man. And let us be clear, the evidence heavily suggests that the system is against you.

Throughout the course of your lifetime as you carry out your activities the racist system controls your every move and decisions-making process whilst you remain in a docile state of unconsciousness.

The systems that we live under are not designed for black people to be self-reliant or prosperous as a collective, but to be controlled and used for the benefit of white people.

You are at the mercy, and under the control of the euro-centric system. You have been fully integrated into it.

And as a result of the colonialist subjugation of said system, you black people are not in control of yourselves, you operate within the system as mentally enslaved individuals not as a unit. The slavery of old is very much alive, my dear brothers and sisters, but it operates within a different format and an altered set of rules.

Is White Supremacy Terrorism?

Let's not be bullied into not being able to speak the truth, or have reversed psychology used upon us that points out that we, black people are racist when we raise the issues of white supremacy and systemic racism.

What you see and live each and every day is the white man's economic power in action through a regime of controlled structures which we voluntarily remain a part of even though the negative outcomes for black people under the system are crystal clear. It's insane!

White supremacy is an arrogant, privileged-entitled system of structures perpetrated by self-imposed rich and powerful people that reign, for their benefit, to conquer, and seize control for world domination. It may sound overly dramatic, but it's true.

From the day we are born and raised into western society our parents rely upon the white dominated systems and structures and we in-turn learn to rely upon them for ourselves and for our children.

The pattern continues through systematic conditioning. Conditioning that began with the African Holocaust, and continues to be embedded in your subconscious mind today. Leading you to believe that you can only survive and, or have access to the riches of the world if you conform as a part of this system.

Within its intricate mechanisms the system conditions you to integrate, in order to control every facet of your life, whilst it conspires against you, fails you, oppresses and slays you.

Make no mistake, the system is purpose built for white success, and black failure. It teaches you, black people, to be irresponsible, to hate yourselves, to have low self-esteem, and to be frivolous.

It keeps you demobilised, ineffective and poor. The system teaches you to operate as an individual not as a unit, to turn you against, and kill your own.

This system is no accident of this society, it didn't just magically appear. It is a well thought out strategy, passed down through generations of people with a clear cut design to execute and sustain white supremacy.

After we, Africans, built up Europe with free labour, sweat and blood, and thereafter slavery was formally abolished, the white society had no intention of surrendering any of its power or wealth to the black man.

So whilst we were singing "free at last, good God almighty," the controllers of the system were scheming to rid themselves of the 'black man' whom they now had no use for since we could no longer be legally held as slaves.

They couldn't kill us off, but they were not about to share all the wealth and power and treat us as equals either, in their minds the power had to be kept where they thought it belonged, with them.

As a result, we have purpose-built euro-centric systems beneficial to white people and detrimental to black people.

Realistically how can one really expect a people that enslaved and applied atrocities to another set of people, to suddenly see said people as equal, and hand them a fair share of riches and wealth?

You cannot, and it is a crazy expectation on the part of black people, but we continue to rely on white people and expect hand-outs from them since the legal abolition of slavery up until the present day.

So is White Supremacy Terrorism? We have to ask the question because white supremacy is a thing, isn't it. It's a controlled set of structures, so within this set of structures, as a people are we being terrorised?

Think for a moment, every time that you hear the term 'white supremacy' is it in a positive context? Does it make you feel good?

Well, the definition of terrorism in the Oxford dictionary is the unlawful use of violence and intimidation, especially against civilians, in the pursuit of political aims.

So the controllers of the system could argue that white supremacy is not terrorism, as the infrastructures of power are executed lawfully under statute, law and order.

An alternative argument however could be to remove the 'unlawful' aspect of the definition, break down the remaining part of it and compare that to the treatment that you as black people experience everyday under the system of white supremacy and I believe you will have your answer.

Is White Supreme?

So what is white supremacy and is white really supreme? A question posed and answered mainly for the benefit of very young readers.

White supremacy is a racist, political and historical collective structure dominated by white people with a belief that white is superior that is used to control you and I. And white is not actually supreme, we are all just made to believe that it is through propaganda and racist systematic programming under the White Order.

We have established that white supremacy is a 'thing' it was created through beliefs and those beliefs are executed under a controlled set of racist structures.

However, people are not actually born racist, people are born into white supremacist and racist systems. Racism itself however is a disease, a learned behaviour, a form of mental illness, if you will. The same way in which normal behaviour can be taught and learned, diseased behaviour can also be taught and learned.

When it is deconstructed, the intricacies of racism can only be deemed as a form of mental illness. For to hate, fear, envy and treat fellow human beings as sub-human, due to the colour of their skin, cannot be considered as normal human behaviour. It is, on the contrary, savage and uncivilised.

Racism cannot be stopped by assimilation and integration into the white euro-centric systems. Racism is far too systemic and ingrained to stop it just like that.

Quite frankly, the only way to stop people acting with sub-human racist behaviour is through a lobotomy, but we can't do that and racism is here to stay so what do we do?

Your alternative to racism therefore is for you to learn how to work around it, and separate yourself from it in order to beat it. Racism and white supremacy are interlinked a complete problem that is delivered by a collective group of people, therefore it requires a collective set of people to erase its affects.

Collective problems require collective solutions, which is the reason you, black people must undergo collective efforts to free yourselves from its affects.

People should realise that there is no blame about racism directed toward any one individual. Racism cannot be effective through an individual alone it is a collective effort.

It is a statement of fact, the system of racism exists, and is executed collectively by people within a system. A system of which we all live by, a system governed by those that believe without a shadow of a doubt that white is supreme and must remain that way.

In order for the systems to be effective they have to be institutional, and enforced through structures, business, industry, politics, policies and processes, every facet of life. The major players under the system are the media, the judiciary, and the police, and we know whomever controls them owns the system. Systems that bind both you and I to a life of indignity, injustice, inequality, brutality.

You have dependency upon a global empire that continues to keep you oppressed and dysfunctional, and in that dysfunctional state we, as a people lack independence, power and wealth.

It cannot be denied that black people as a collective are disorganised and poor, due to our current state of dependency upon the euro-centric system.

This euro-centric system is the new slavery, and we, you and I, are the subjects of its cruelty. We are the human resource, the commodities that keep it alive.

Agents of the System

Any system, in order to operate effectively must have an operation of execution and channels in which they facilitate. The same applies to the euro-centric system that you currently live by, and the beliefs and principles of that system are executed by people. In slavery days they were called overseers, but today, in the twenty-first century they should be known as agents.

Why agents you ask? Reason being there has been a restructure from eighteenth century slavery to modern day slavery. Just like in any business when the business changes hands, the job-titles change but the objective of the business remains the same, so the overseers have now become agents.

Agents are at different levels in the white power structure and have varying roles. There are top agents that wield the ultimate power and will annihilate anyone who threatens its stability and existence.

The assassination of all the previous out-spoken prominent US Black leaders are a testament to that. As is the UK's ban of entry on leaders that they believe will further the liberation of black people, such as Louis Farrakhan since 1986, citing his threat to public order, is also the work of top level agents.

And let us not forget the white-american savages; Ku Klux Klan, whom consider black people in general a threat to the white order of the USA, and murder at will as a result.

Let us also not forget that the KKK and the US Government are one and the same. Don't be fooled into thinking that the KKK just consists of dumb-ass trailer trash, no, some high ranking officials and business people are at the helm of the KKK. That is the reason for the face covering, they do not want their identity revealed.

There are also agents of the state who execute violence and brutality through the pretext of law enforcement. The countless slaying of black men and women at the hands of police forces are also a testament to that.

The agents in a different part of the spectrum for example those in corporate decision-making positions, use termination of livelihood, the dangling carrot of employment, as a stick to wield power over black people that threaten the systems stability.

And let us not forget the media agents that use propaganda tactics to brainwash the masses on a grand scale under the principles of white supremacy and racism.

The systematic programming of 'white is supreme' is so profound, that agents protect and defend the system at all costs, almost like emotionless robots. There is no logical rationale behind the actions, just a desire to protect, and that my people is high level programming.

Anyone showing any inclination of thinking for him or herself becomes a threat to the stability and existence of the system, which is an automatic cue for the executing agents to act. You will see agents executing their responsibilities through the corporate plantation institutions whether it be the celebrity plantation of the rich and famous or the poor everyday lifestyle of the nine to fivers.

The Corporate Plantation

I must confess I first heard the term 'corporate plantation' used by an American brother, and I found it both amusing and fitting that I now use the term myself.

We are modern day slaves on a corporate plantation. Agents of the system govern the corporate plantation, that you work for, and you, as a black person have zero power. You are the commodity working for the leaders of that plantation, and they get rich off you.

As a modern day slave and commodity, the only difference between the sixteenth-eighteenth slave plantation and the current corporate plantation is that you get paid for the work that you do and you cannot be legally physically whipped.

However, you cannot say how that plantation is run, you cannot employ a group of people that look like you, you cannot own any part of the plantation, you cannot get rich by working on the plantation.

You will not be allowed to do anything that will progress the collective power of your people. It is their system and their rules apply for them to win.

On the plantation during the African Holocaust hair of the black woman was hated, and a rule was not to offend the Massa. Therefore our ancestors were made to act in accordance with the rules so as not to offend the Massa which meant covering or wrapping of our hair.

Things have not particularly changed in the twenty-first century as we have seen media reports of black women both in the UK and the US, with locks and other natural hair styles being denied access to corporate plantation jobs.

The denial of plantation entry also occurs in educational institutions where boys and girls have been suspended due to hairstyles exclusive to black people, such as afros and cornrows which are deemed offensive to the systems agents.

These are actions of agents exercising today's unwritten plantation rules, establishing their power and control to do as they will, which includes preventing your entry into their corporations when they are overcome by their feelings of black fear and racism.

The conditioned feelings of racism and so called white supremacy as we know it, is what drives the mainstream behaviour thus maintaining oppression and subjugation.

The black woman hiding and masking her hair is still prevalent in today's society, although with the denial of the black woman's hair in corporate plantations becoming so wide-spread, movements have been established by young girls and women alike across the globe celebrating the natural hair of the black woman which is fantastic!

However looking at the denial of access to the plantation through your hair is one aspect of the work of the agents power and control to demonstrate to you that you are allowed into their plantation within the rules of their authorisation.

You are made to feel dependancy towards working within the system of the corporate plantation, including the need to change in order to be accepted onto the plantation as you have no other alternative.

So even though you are treated bad you still stay within the system because you are programmed that way, and that is the control that we are having difficulty escaping from.

We are being controlled every step of the way, and when you really analyse the system, I mean sit down, tear it apart and analyse it for what it really is. What is revealed is some sick mind twisting crazy bull….!!!

Whilst these are clearly racist acts on the part of the system, and the law seemingly gives you the right to challenge such acts. You should ask yourself whether you really want to spend the best part of your life in an environment where your hair, an extension of your culture and who you are is deemed as a negative?

Do you really want to beg to be included and accepted in an environment where people can make you feel so bad about your hair that you no longer want it. Think about it.

Double Agents

Did you know that there are also members of the black community that operate as agents. It's almost like watching a spy film, where you have the spy playing two-sides, hence the term, double agent.

Black agents defend and justify their place in the system as they know no other alternative and see being part of the system as the only option of survival.

Falling prey to conditioning, some black agents operate behind the scenes and have sold out the likes of Malcolm X whilst pretending to support the black cause.

Others at different levels within the system will be more overt and cry out, against an alternative black economic system for their own black people, they oppose self reliance and black liberation.

They support integration, and the right for more jobs in the corporate plantation. They fight for recognition and respect to be given to them by their oppressors for which they believe will be their great salvation. That is serious programming right there!

Some of us as black people have become so comfortable, in our jobs and lifestyle, with our money or celebrity status, that we ignore the fact that we are living within an evil regime of white supremacist systems. Remember, we have established that it exists.

You must also remember that you are allowed to live within it, just as long as you live by the rules, do as you are told and do not try to alter the systems mechanisms or principles.

So why are we in denial? Why do we walk around blind to the realities and put up with what the system spits out at us?

We know and feel it every day as the system degrades us, inflicts physical pain upon us, we suffer humiliation and submissiveness yet still we stay a part of it, in fact we beg to be included in it like little children.

I am sorry but in one word I can only describe this behaviour as masochistic. And I would really like to know what you describe this behaviour as in one word.

For those of us whom are not in denial of what the system is, and we no longer want to be masochistic we are prevented from talking about white supremacy and euro-centric systematic oppression not only to white people but amongst ourselves.

When it is suggested that liberation is the way forward from a system that beguiles us we are attacked and prevented from discussing self-reliance as an option for escape.

The issue of black liberation was raised by me on social media, and not in any real depth, I was responding to a post about integration. However that was the cue for the agents of the system to act.

Never mind the fact that I was not addressing them, they felt the need to poke their noses where it did not belong, and acted exactly as any agent of the system would.

They switched the situation and called me racist. And I quote "the biggest racist in the thread." Oh yeaah! That was said when I put forward views that black people should be self-reliant and create industries for themselves and should not depend upon the white power structure.

"You blame others for racism and yet you advocate 'segregation' and 'division'?? Unbelievable." One said. "Tarring the whole entertainment industry with the 'white supremacist' brush doesn't help, I take deep offence to being branded a problem just because of the colour of my skin." Said another.

These are real statements made when I commented that the actor Idris Elba's plea for more diversity in the creative arts, was not the answer, but creating our own film industry, independence and self-reliance for black people is the answer.

White people do not have the right to accuse anybody of racism, when their race has been perpetuating racism on nations of people over centuries on a grand scale.

They should refrain from expressing views on social media threads regarding issues affecting black people, crying 'racism,' and suggesting that integration is the best way forward for us.

These actions are just another example of what is the arrogance of white supremacy. White people want to continue to tell black people what they should and should not do as they did during the African Holocaust.

In the first social media statement you can see how they protect the system. Firstly by clouding the principles of self-reliance and segregation of which they are different.

And by the same token advocating integration as the answer to end racism, whilst implying that segregation and division is not the answer to end racism.

Remember in the preface we discussed the meaning of self-reliance, being economic control. Self-reliance and separation is very different to segregation and I do not advocate segregation.

The white power structure knows there is a difference, and is afraid of the black man becoming self-reliant because then you will be out of his control. His commodities gone clear! Finished!

Segregation means that which is forced upon inferiors by superiors. A segregated community is a black community. South Africa is an example of segregation and I most certainly do not advocate that.

The white community, though it's all white, is never called a segregated community, it's a separate community.

In the white community, the white man controls the economy, his own economy, his own politics, his own everything. That's his community, but at the same time while the black man lives in a separate community, it's a segregated community which means it's regulated from the outside by outsiders. The white man has all of the businesses in the black community. He runs the politics of the black community. He controls all the civic organisations in the black community, the politics and the economy. This is a segregated community.

As black people we already have segregated communities, this is not what we want, we want separate communities. There is a vast difference.

An example of that segregation is the current black housing estate areas and the interlinked white power infrastructure as the controller. In matters of social housing, the rules of integration do not apply. We are segregated from white people and all thrown together in housing estates that are economically starved, neglected and turned into ghettos of depravation, from which we are conditioned to run drugs and undertake criminal activity as a means to obtain wealth.

The agents advocate integration in order that you stay within control, and also muddle self-reliance with segregation in order to confuse the masses.

It is important that you are not distracted or fooled by the psychological warfare confusing the meanings of words.

The second statement on social media showed the person explaining that they took offence to being branded a problem because of the colour of their skin.

Are you kidding me with that statement? It seems to me that white people cannot take what they dish out. Remember we spoke of negative associations with 'black' in the introduction.

For centuries through propaganda black people have been branded savages and a problem because of the colour of their skin and we have been made to put up with it.

Anyway, my comments on social media were defended by many, the following by a conscious black brother, Nicholas Estephane,was most poignant. The thing that I find most amusing (as expected)!.... Are all the white profile pictures coming here to accuse Khadijah Ward of being racist and promoting segregation. Self reliance and segregation are world's apart. I've been in the unfortunate position of trying to explain the system of racism to certain white people on numerous occasions... It truly is like banging your head against a brick wall. Khadijah, I couldn't agree with you more, self reliance all the way!

The black nation needs millions more like-minded people like the brother who made the above comments, it is that type of mind-set that will enable the black community to unite and become self-reliant to develop as productive wealthy communities.

When white people call a black person racist it is a reversed psychology tactic, that will scare some black people into going against their own in support of the regime, and it works.

On the social media, various comments were made in support of integration into the racist system. One comment made by an individual with a black profile, a double agent, who said;

“There's only one image a human being is in and it's neither black nor white non anything in between, and also....You're talking about building walls...when Black ppl respond to perceived racism by segregating themselves further it just perpetuates racism, which is based on separation. That isn't the answer.”

Notice the reference to being colour blind, seeing people as just ‘human beings.’ A ridiculous and ignorant notion, as it is not possible in a society where the colour of your skin is the first thing that people see, and that colour is used as a weapon against you to determine your treatment.

The use of the word ‘perceived’ next to racism implies that racism does not exist.

Using separation as a negative to champion integration into the system as a positive without actually using the word integration, although that is clearly what the statement suggests.

This individual’s comments also demonstrate that he is a double agent. Completely programmed and fooled by the white person’s comments about ‘advocating segregation.’

He has been conditioned to believe that self-reliance is the same as segregation and that the best way forward for black people is within the euro-centric system.

Remember, we referred to black 'double' agents that defend the system. These are the type of statements you will hear from such agents. They will fight for integration to remain a part of the system and are completely and utterly blind to the damage towards the black community for integrating within a euro-centric system.

These type of people will never believe in black liberation unless the white power structure, their controllers, gives them permission to do so, and that will never happen. They, my brothers and sisters are the lost causes of our people that sadly will be left behind.

"Not all white people are racist" - Null and Void – Mohammed Ali

There are some white people that sympathise with the plight of black people, and have campaigned and picketed alongside us over the years, great! And those people have been welcomed with open arms and commended for their support.

So those type of people tend to get defensive when issues of white supremacy are raised, and take offence at the suggestion that white people are racist. As one of the social media comments stated; "I take deep offence to being branded a problem just because of the colour of my skin." Isn't that exactly how black people are seen?

As Muhammed Ali the outspoken boxer and activist eloquently put it, during an interview on the British chat show Parkinson, in 1971. The argument of "not all white people are racist" will always be null and void. Here is what he said.

"There are many white people who mean right and in their hearts wanna do right, but If 10,000 snakes were coming down that aisle now, and I had a door that I could shut, and in that 10,000, 1,000 meant right, 1,000 rattlesnakes didn't want to bite me, I knew they were good... Should I let all these rattlesnakes come down, hoping that the thousand get together and form a shield? Or should I just close the door and stay safe?"

Ali went on to say... "so now I'm going to forget the 400 years of killing, lynching and raping and deprive my people of freedom, justice, equality, seen as the lowest of the low, least respected, and I'm going to look at two or three white people who are trying to do right and don't see the other million who are trying to kill me..., I'm not that big of a fool."

For the record, it is not the responsibility of black people to pander to the feelings of a handful of white people that take offence when issues surrounding what is known as white supremacy are raised. The issues are much bigger than the feelings of people of other races that may be trying to help.

Black people are being jailed, oppressed, brutalised and murdered on a daily basis through this white supremacist system that people fight so hard to keep us in.

We cannot be concerned with the feelings of people that considered themselves good samaritans or 'not racist' as that is a distraction from the real issues of obtaining liberation and self-reliance.

Black people are affected by racism in a manner which white people could not begin to understand, therefore they have no authority to say what is best for black people.

They do not share our experiences, and therefore have no idea what is best for you or I. You have to live and breath racism to the extent that black people have over centuries, to fully understand its devastating affects.

Even those of us whom have financially benefited from the system, remember small pockets of us are allowed to benefit at the say so of the system controllers, will still experience the negative impact of the system.

Let's be clear, the euro-centric system is racist, and even black billionaires integrated within the system will experience racism.

Black Celebrities

Mike Tyson, Michael Jackson, Muhammed Ali, Bill Cosby, and some basketball players are just a few celebrities that were allowed to benefit financially from the system but then tried to step outside of what they were allowed to do and suffered extreme consequences.

Michael Jackson's (MJ) power over the people was very scary for the system. He had a movement of people at his command, if he said jump people would say how high.

Clearly that was too much power for a black man, he had to go. However, if MJ was operating within a black economic system, with groups of other 'MJ' types the likelihood of him being taken out would be considerably reduced. As it stands he was operating within the euro-centric system that enabled him to rise therefore there are limitations to what he is able to do due to not being a controller of that system, and his limit was reached when he tried to do particular things.

When Billionaire Media mogul Oprah Winfrey asked to see a bag in an expensive shop in Zurich, the shop assistant said "No, no, no, you don't want to see that one, because that one will cost too much, you will not be able to afford that one". Winfrey said the assistant ultimately refused to get the bag in question. A lowly shop assistant thought that she was better than a black woman customer who in her mind could not possible afford a bag priced at $38,000.

When it came to light in the media the owner of the store said her assistant was not racist and did not do anything wrong, which in my view is not a surprising conclusion to reach as standard agent operation is to protect and defend the racist behaviour of one another.

Actually it was a racist act, as what racist people fail to admit is that part of racism is perception. Individuals are judged based on what someone of a particular race is perceived to be and are treated in accordance with that perception. So yes miss 'old hag' shop owner you and your lowly assistant are both racist, but personally speaking I would not even consider giving you $38,000 of my money in the first place.

If black people were an economic group to be reckoned with, we would have our own expensive handbag stores to shop in and our own film industries to recruit our own in thus eliminating the possibility of experiencing racism. Readers are you getting this?

We need the millionaires and billionaires to unite with ordinary people and give money to create institutions, industries and jobs to enable others to escape the system and start building for self-reliance. Instead we find most of those in a privileged positions acting like brain-washed morons.

The Oscars Have a Right to Promote Only White

The Jada Pinkett-Smith saga in 2016 saw her publicly complain regarding a lack of diversity for the Oscar awards. This was an example of 'black agent' type behaviour, whereby she fought for and defended her integrated oppressed state.

As an integrated member of the system, she feels an entitlement to be included. And as she had not been included in the Oscar nominations, she proceeded to beg for inclusion, acceptance and self-worth as it were, through a public campaign, with a desired outcome to be recognised by the Oscar's power structure, a dominant white power structure.

Jada PS, and other such celebrities should not be begging for acceptance and campaigning about the Oscars lack of black celebrities, after all, it is a white industry and only naturally they will recognise and elevate their own people.

There is nothing wrong with the oscars promoting only white people, it is their creation. What is wrong is that black people are begging to be part of their action? Please, stop the public begging it's humiliating. Get your own!

Black celebrities should focus on how they can invest their multi-millions to build black empires that up-lifts their brothers and sisters who are at the lower ends of the system, suffering, being jailed or murdered, or just simply scrambling for a job opportunity.

Many black celebrities in the film, sports and music industries have integrated with the system and accumulated massive amounts of wealth. Therefore, they are in the perfect position to donate their wealth and build industries and create jobs and opportunities for black people, but they do not.

They move into the white man's neighbourhood and forget the suffering masses, their brothers and sisters, or about creating black industry. They just continue to beg for more and more of the white man's action.

The mechanics and the effectiveness of the system are apparent from this one example of the Pinkett saga. Black people integrated within the system do not have power of any sort.

Some of us, like the celebrities will be allowed tiny pockets of infiltration, to excel through industries with accumulated wealth, but with that wealth and false status comes a price. The price being at the expense of your people and the surrender of your personal power.

When you are a part of the system, you must abide by the rules of the system to keep that wealth, but that wealth does not grant you powers to make unilateral changes.

You are not in control of that system no matter how much money you may have. You are merely a temporary guest in the house of the slave master.

Power can only be created through building self-reliant structure and systems. If wealthy black people combine their wealth, and that wealth is then transferred to building industry and commerce that is owned and run by people for and within that community, only then will power be achieved.

This methodology works, simply because the principles of the structure and systems are created in the best interests of the people for whom it is aimed to benefit.

A prime example is the euro-centric systems that we live under. White people are in charge, white people have the power, white people make the decisions, white people have the wealth and white people benefit from the system. Fact!

Black people need to build the self-reliant structures and systems to create power and control over what they can and cannot do. If they do not, then it will continue on as Pinkett-Smith sagas, where black people not only beg for inclusion and recognition, but will forever be reliant upon systems that perpetrate our ultimate destruction.

As Kwame Ture quite rightly said, "The system is for you or against you there is no middle ground." Tell me what you think, is the system for you or against you? From the Cradle to the Jail, read on...

CHAPTER 2

FROM THE CRADLE TO THE JAIL

"*The Black Man, the African, is the real leader of the world. So, when the system removes him from the equation. the family, you are left with a disabled community that cannot function. As females we must support and elevate the black man to reach his rightful place as the leader of our nation and indeed the world*" – Khadijah Ward

A Broken Unit

I have vivid memories of the days as a child when my mother and father were married and I belonged to a family. Happy times. Until my parents divorced when I was fifteen years old, thereafter my emotional well-being took a dive.

We all need a mother and a father, as each parent has a specific role to play in the raising of the child and the family unit which should consist of two parents is so very important to the stability and physiological well-being of children.

So when a parent is absent, let's say the father for argument sake, that unit becomes broken and shattered, as the leader of the unit is now not around to lead which consequently has a high probability of a negative impact upon the child's emotional development.

So when I saw the UK Government statistics in 2010 that said seven out of ten offenders come from broken homes, and that, single parent families were more than twice as likely to live in poverty than those living with both parents, I was not surprised, I viewed it as results of an oppressive system.

Previously I ran a business that dealt with the rehabilitation of young offenders and I found that eight out of ten of the offenders that crossed my path were black and from single parent families. Again, this is what the system creates and churns out.

The Odds are Against Them

When we have children we imagine a perfect family of a husband and wife and how we want our children's life to turn out.

We dream of that child being the next 'big thing' or we just simply want them to be happy and successful. How we categorise success may differ from one to another, but we all want our children to do well in their life journey that is a given.

Nobody dreams of their child being a product of a single parent family, being homeless, poor, on drugs or incarcerated. So what do we do? We give them the start that we hope will help them on their way to the 'promised land' starting with the institution of school. A fact of which we have a legal obligation toward in this society.

And so the journey begins, we send them to school to do well, get qualifications, go to college and university get qualifications, get a good job, get married start a family of their own.

That is the conditioning of the system that we have had as being the right thing to do. So we project that conditioning upon our children and put them through the same, but wait a minute, have we informed them what to expect? And that the odds are against them every step of the way.

The statistics around attainment and school exclusion are suggestive of a racist system that grooms black children for a life of crime, and or under-achievers that will lead to an unproductive lifestyle with no wealth.

Have we informed them of these statistics, and those that relate to children from single parent families? Have we informed them that black children in the UK are labelled as disruptive trouble makers and are four times more likely than any other group to be permanently excluded from school?

Have we informed them that the school system is designed to rip apart their self-esteem and set them up to fail? No, we have not. We have all of the information before us and yet we still send our children down the garden path to the hell hole of fate.

Remember when we spoke of the intricacies of the system being enforced through industries and policy and other structural channels.

Well, your education institutions and I say your, because that is the system that you rely upon to educate your children, is another one of the components within the larger system, and it has specific duties to assist with achieving the overall objective of the system.

My first born child, exceptionally intelligent, actually like a grown man in a child's body, with leadership qualities displayed as young as three years old. Yet somehow he was deemed a trouble maker and eventually permanently excluded from school.

You know the story right. I can bet that each and every one of you know somebody who's child has been permanently excluded, or your own child may even have been excluded from school.

The education system treats white children very differently to that of black children. Black children are simply not treated well, or encouraged to succeed, or taught about our great black history of royalty, Kings, Queens, Warriors and Creators. Black children are systematically taught that we are lesser human beings and our history began with slavery.

I remember an incident in school made me feel not so good about myself at eleven years old in a classroom of white children, myself and another child being the only two black children.

We were being taught about slavery, and the teacher used a female slave in a book as an example of what ignorance and uneducated looks like. She actually asked the class to tell her how could we tell the slave, wasn't educated. The audacity of the agents of the system is unprecedented.

In my view the overall purpose of an education institutions is to educate children to function as productive adults in society. The curriculum should include subjects to help them function in the real world to include their real history, heritage and heroes. Including encouraging confidence greatness and leadership to enable a child to succeed. The current curriculum of Math, English, Science and Geography accompanied by back-stabbing racist tactics is not the answer to the education of next generation black leaders.

Children are the next generation of rulers, therefore teaching them to feel good about themselves to help them to succeed is the duty of any education system together with the parents.

The white education system does just that, for its white children. It teaches 'white history' as all powerful and great; William the Conquerer, Alexander 'the Great,' Christopher Columbus, poets, playwrights, inventors and so on, these teachings help the white child to feel good about him or her self and instil confidence in him which is an integral ingredient to success.

Ask your child if he or she has been taught about, or even knows of the great African civilisation and its royalty. Or the African origins of Math, Astronomy, Metallurgy and tools, Architecture and engineering, Medicine, and Navigation from across Africa.

The euro-centric education system does not teach about the real African history, not only because that would instil a sense of leadership and pride in black children, but it would reveal the truth regarding the black man's sophisticated and superior civilisation which is not conducive to the supremacist regime.

The education system is in essence a preparation course for both a path of greatness and crime. White children to be great adults and winners, and black children to be adult criminals and losers. Its simple math, one add one equals two.

You only have to look at the negative statistics that dominate the black community, of unemployment, crime, drug dealing and abuse and poverty to see the end result of a western education system.

If the majority of the black population are on drugs, dealing drugs, undertaking other criminal activity, in prison or dead through killing each other or through interactions with law enforcement, it is not possible to educate and nurture rulers, build industry, create wealth, a black economy no less, where our children and our people prosper, are wealthy and live happy and productive lives.

Unemployment carries a nothing existence and the undertaking of criminal activity carries a high risk of imprisonment. Unemployed people cannot contribute to a black economy, and incarcerated individuals are absent and unproductive members of the community.

Incarceration prevents people from creating family units, setting examples of leadership, and contributing to building industry and wealth of the black community.

Don't Blame the Children

Our unemployed and incarcerated people are products of an organised system which starts from the school institution and continues on throughout adulthood.

With black children being excluded from school, and mixed-raced children too, as they are no exception to the rule being seen as black in the eyes of the system. There is an increased likelihood of becoming a school drop-out and entering the path of crime, as poor or little education leads to reduced prospects for the future, so the immediate options for such children would be either a dead end job or a life of crime.

Even though we are aware of how our children are treated as inferior, and they are conditioned through the school system to ultimately become failures, we as adults and leaders of our children have not taken the responsibility to create educational institutions for their needs.

Children that grow up to become unproductive members of society cannot be blamed for their plight. You and I are to blame, as we have failed to provide an economic system conducive to their needs for which they may thrive. We have literally led them to their demise.

The destructive activities that the black community currently experience under the system ensure that we will die prematurely, remain trapped in poverty or be incarcerated unless we as a community make a change.

Slave to the Plantation Wage

And for those of your children whom manage to pass through the education system with qualifications and such, simply become slaves to the system, which essentially means they will be 'pimped out' to the corporate plantation for the slave wage, in the process of which the white corporations become wealthy.

Some individuals may become comfortable with a nice lifestyle but the communities that your brothers and sisters live in are not sharing the same wealth and lifestyle as those individuals.

Whilst you are working for the corporate plantations to build their wealth and obtain your own individual lifestyle, the money from the corporations is spent making white communities wealthy and black communities remain poor because white communities and other communities for that matter spend their money with their own communities and nobody is spending in the black community.

Tell me, how much money of the corporate plantation's wealth that you help them build, do you think goes into building the black community? A big fat zero! That is the answer. White corporations make white communities rich. You go through the education system to work for white corporations to make them rich.

It's a conveyor belt of people, a win-win for the system, just like slavery. In slavery we worked for the slave masters we had no choice and our lives had no other direction but to exist upon the whim of the slave owners. The slave owners received free labour and got rich in the process, and in return we relied upon them to give us the basics, shelter, clothing and food.

Now, in the modern day, you work for the corporate plantation through choice. The difference is they pay you a salary so that you can pay for your own shelter, clothing and food however you are still reliant upon their systems for your shelter and food, and without their salary you would have no shelter, food or clothing.

The clothes you buy are mainly from white-owned businesses right? The food you buy is mainly from white-owned supermarkets right? The houses you live in are from the government owned council estates, right? Or the houses you have that are by mortgage is money borrowed from white-owned banks, right?And the fact that these are our only choices is our own fault.

You see we have been blindly led down the garden path. We have been allowed to integrate the system because the controllers do not want us running off and creating our own systems they want us as slaves and under control to maintain power, they do not want us as competitors.

However we are still slaves and not competitors, evidently we are still reliant on the corporate plantation for all of our needs.

Let me give you hypothetical, if a law was passed tomorrow that said we are no longer housing black people on our council estates, we are not lending black people money for mortgages, we are not allowing black people to shop in our supermarkets, we are not allowing black people to work on our corporate plantations. How would you survive?

Do you see what I am getting at, you are at the mercy of someone else infrastructures and systems, they have the power and pull the strings, and if they decided to pull the plug on you, you would be left up the creek without a paddle.

Conveyor Belt Links

There are links within the systems chain that ensures your life of a broken home, low education, crime, incarceration, poverty and ultimate demise as black people.

We blindly rely upon the euro-centric power structure to meet our needs within every facet of the system which is the major part of the black mans downfall.

The undertaking of criminal activity carries a risk of imprisonment, and incarcerated individuals are absent and unproductive members of the community. Incarceration prevents people from creating family units, setting examples of leadership, and contributing to building industry and wealth of the black community.

Regarding recent statistics on exclusion of black boys from schools, I could not find any statistics. The government has purposely lumped every one of colour together with an addendum that reads pupils with a black or mixed ethnic background were more likely to be excluded than their white counterparts.

That lame statement covers up the awful truth of how their education system just throws our children out of school at the drop of a hat and on to the unemployment line.

In 2012, the Office of National Statistics produced data that showed half of the UK's Black males were unemployed aged 16-24. In 2015 they showed a 50% rise in long term unemployment for young ethnic minority people age 16-24.

These figures are for Black and Asian people, the system has a tendency of lumping us all together, but we do know that black unemployment is twice as high than that of white children. This is the result of integrating within a system that is designed to work against you.

Pretext of Law and Order

From poor education and school exclusion the conveyor belt of black destruction, progresses to victims of murder under the law, another link in the system's chain of judge, jury and executioner.

Police forces whom are agents, of the State, the power structure, enforce oppression, domination, and inflict violence through legitimate means, that is the law.

The justification of police forces treatment towards the black community stems from the 'black fear' syndrome that we discussed earlier in the introduction, which provides for the introduction of laws and policies to satisfy the fear and wipe out the black population.

In the US a fictional 'war on drugs' government policy was used to escalate the incarceration of the black population.

A Nixon administrative official admitted that the war on drugs was about throwing black people in jail.

He said " The Nixon campaign in 1968, and the Nixon White House after that, had two enemies: the antiwar left and black people. You understand what I'm saying? We knew we couldn't make it illegal to be either against the war or black...

but by getting the public to associate the hippies with marijuana and blacks with heroin, and then criminalising both heavily, we could disrupt those communities…

We could arrest their leaders, raid their homes, break up their meetings, and vilify them night after night on the evening news. Did we know we were lying about the drugs? Of course we did."

In the nineties Bill Clinton and his administration's attitude towards crime was far worse than his predecessors. He is responsible for the militarisation of the police force infrastructure that Americans see today.

He pushed the 1994 $30 billion dollar crime bill which was heavily loaded toward law enforcement and incarceration, that saw a massive expansion of the prison system money to build prisons to lock up people involved in drug crimes, and led to a surge in the imprisonment of black people.

The policy put 100,000 more police on the streets, introduced mandatory minimums, the California '3 strikes and you are out' law which means on your third felony you are mandated to prison of the rest of your life, truth in sentencing which means you serve 85% of your time.

The US prison/correction service is heavily monetised with partnerships between it and private businesses which profit from mass incarceration and prison labour, a massive multibillion dollar industry.

These racist laws and policies forced families to be broken and children to live without their parents. That is the monster of the systems of oppression that we live under.

A World-Wide System

The UK operates under the same systems as the US with some minor differences in execution. In the UK police officers have powers to stop and search you if they have 'reasonable grounds' to suspect you're carrying: illegal drugs, a weapon or stolen property.

Under the pretext of law and order the harassment of the black community begins with the disproportionate implementation of police forces Stop and Search powers.

The fact that black youths are seven times more likely to be stopped and searched by police more than white people (Asian youths are four times more likely), is not just simple harassment in isolation.

It is one element of the bigger system a grooming preparation, a means to introduce youths to a smooth transition through the criminal justice system and the ultimate justified means of murder under the law 'Shoot to Kill' on the pretext that the black male or female was a criminal, or a member of a gang.

Since 1990, there has been nine unlawful killing verdicts returned by juries at inquests into deaths involving the police and one unlawful killing verdict recorded by a public inquiry, none of which has yet resulted in a successful prosecution, as reported by the Institute of Race Relations, a UK based Charity.

More than 500 black and so called 'ethnic minority' individuals have died in suspicious circumstances while in state detention over the past 24 years, but not a single official has been successfully prosecuted, a report examining institutional racism has revealed.

More than 1,000 deaths in custody, and not one successful prosecution of a single police officer, despite a verdict of unlawful killing in several instances, or a verdict handed down only after years, or even decades, of work, campaigning and painstaking legal challenges by the families of those killed.

The list of those who've died has grown ever longer, as does the gap between now and the last time a police officer was prosecuted for the death of somebody in custody.

That record stretches back 48 years to 1969, when the two officers who were implicated in the death of David Oluywale, the first black man to die in police custody in the UK, were found guilty of assault and sentenced to a pitiful few months in prison.

People, please take a moment to remember our UK brothers and sisters that have died at the hands of the system's agents:

The afore-mentioned David Oluyawale (1969), Colin Roach, (1983), Dorothy "Cherry" Groce (1985), Cynthia Jarrett (1985), Christopher Ibikunle Alder, (1998), Azelle Rodney, (2005), Sean Rigg, (2008), Smiley Culture (2011) Mark Duggan, (2011), Sarah Reid (2016) Edson Da Costa (2017), Rashan Charles (2017), Darren Cumberbatch (2017) to name a few.

A Deadly Tool

Before we even reach the criminal justice stage, that is the legal stage in which a child can be prosecuted, we are groomed through education — school, to ensure that the majority of you lead a life that would naturally see you enter the criminal justice system through the slightest infraction in the white social order.

The Prison Reform Trust reports, 21,937 prisoners from a minority ethnic group. This compares to around one in 10 of the general population.

Overall Black prisoners account for the largest number of minority ethnic prisoners (49%). Out of the British national prison population. 10% are Black and 6% are Asian. For black Britons this is significantly higher than the 2.8% of the general population they represent.

These statistics aren't due to black men being 'bad men' or natural born criminals, this is a system of racism in action. A system rooted in centuries of capitalism and colonialism beginning with the African Holocaust, also known as the Trans-Atlantic Slave Trade.

We have seen how the agents of the power structure enforce oppression through domination, and inflict discrimination harassment and violence through institutional systems. Well, the criminal justice system, is one of, if not the most deadly of tools within the White Social Order.

The criminal justice system was originally created to exercise law and order of the general masses which appears as legitimate systems of law enforcement and the judiciary.

When in fact it is an inherently racist criminal justice system where racism is systematically enforced to denigrate and destroy the black man, whilst in the process he is also used as an economic commodity.

Remember that racism is a learned behaviour, and that learned behaviour is executed by the agents of said behaviour like emotionless robots. These behaviours ensure that black males are over-represented at almost every stage of the criminal justice process, disproportionately targeted by police forces, the legitimised agents of the regime.

The council estates and highly populated black areas are purposely segregated and economically starved to encourage unsavoury behaviour. Where there is poverty, high unemployment and little prospects in life, there is the increased likelihood of criminal activity.

The UK government has presented these statistics through the media which provides the masses with an expectation of behaviour, and in turn legitimises any action taken on the part of the state to eliminate possible criminal activity.

Some of you may remember back in 1995 The Metropolitan Police's controversial campaign against street crime, 'Operation Eagle Eye.' Instigated by the then Sir Paul Condon, Chief of Britain's largest police force public declaration that "80% of street muggings in London are committed by black men."

His statement that community leaders must "grasp the nettle" and recognise the problem of street crime brought immediate condemnation from London's black members of Parliament.

"People will just think that every young black person is a mugger because the metropolitan police commissioner says it is so," said lawmaker Bernie Grant. Paul Boateng, another legislator who received Condon's letter, attacked its message as "unhelpful" and challenged police statistics.

You can clearly see how the propaganda of 'black fear' is used through the system of the media. To link mugging with race sends fear into the minds of the white population, it makes black men appear as criminals, and it gives the justification to target black men through the criminal justice system with campaigns such as 'operation eagle eye' Are you getting this people?

We have witnessed police forces swarm upon black areas and harass your children, as by their perception, there is a high possibility that crimes will be committed.

Black people are more likely to be imprisoned, and more likely to be imprisoned for longer than white British people. The number of black people jailed in England and Wales is seven times larger than the amount they make up of the population. This unfair and dare I say racist decision-making in the judiciary was witnessed by a black magistrate, Iris Josiah.

In a civil law case Iris Josiah v Ministry of Justice

Black female magistrate Iris Josiah claimed racist judges tried to force her out of her job as a magistrate after she highlighted alleged racist treatment of black defendants.

She alleged her fellow lay justices were routinely 'hostile' towards black people and convicted them on slim or no evidence.

The magistrate added that black people were also jailed for longer terms and were more likely to be sent to prison and refused bail than white defendants.

Ms. Josiah was unlawfully suspended by court bosses after voicing her concerns about her colleagues' racism.

In the next section of this book 'My Story is Your Story' I explain to you that I learned even if a few token black people are placed in prominent positions we still cannot stop the racism from inside of the system.

Well, Ms Josiah's case is a perfect example of that. The system will work and enforce racism whether black people are present in prominent positions or not. Black people are only in such positions as tokens, and no more, they exercise no power over how the system is applied to black people.

White colleagues will apply racist decision-making right under your very nose and you will be powerless to stop it as we have seen so many times before. As I explain later in the book there are repercussions for upsetting the system, just ask Magistrate Ms Josiah.

The Central Park Five

The central park five relates to our brothers and sisters in the US, and is a perfect example of just how racist the criminal justice system is world-wide. And that you as black people will never be treated fairly or have your innate rights as a human being recognised.

You are despised by the controllers of the system, but you need not take my word for it just take a look at the way that your brothers and sisters are treated as evidence enough of a system of hate.

This heart-breaking story involved five boys, four black and one latino from Harlem ranged from the ages of 14-16. Korey Wise; Kevin Richardson, Yusef Salaam, Raymond Santana, and Antron McCray were wrongly accused and convicted of raping a white women in central park in 1989.

The brutal beating and rape of a white woman in New York City's Central Park provoked public outrage and sensational headlines during the prosecution and conviction of the five boys.

From the spectacle of their arrest to the farce of their trial that came across as a human zoo. They were treated like animals by the prosecutor at the time, coerced confessions and their rights violated by the police was just the tip of the ice-berg of the trauma faced by these five young boys.

The filthy KKK sympathiser pig Donald Trump took out a four-page advert in a newspaper calling for the death penalty to be brought back specifically for these young boys.

They were eventually exonerated after serving their full sentences, and the reporting of their exoneration was low key when it came to light the crime had been committed by someone else. However that did not stop Trump from again going public opposing the $40 million-suit that they received from the city.

The victim being a white woman and the accused being black males means that the innocent until proven guilty does not apply. Black males are deemed guilty first and the system will take you through its process and you will be found guilty under their court of law nine times out of ten.

The central park five story has been called a miscarriage of justice, but it isn't that. The justice was carried out exactly as the agents of the system wanted it to be carried out. A guilty verdict and the lives of black males and the family ruined.

Prison Commodities

For centuries the black man has been a human resource for the white power structure, and since the Slave Trade, prison has long since been an expectation of life, and a reality nightmare shared by black males all over Europe and the US.

Black males (and females) were traded as commodities in the slave economy, whereby white slave owners, slave traders and their dependents built and inherited vast family fortunes on the sweat, blood and free labour of enslaved Africans.

Slavery, on an industrial scale was a major source of the wealth of the British empire. As many as one-fifth of wealthy Victorian Britons derived all or part of their fortunes from the slave economy. As a result, there are now wealthy families all around the UK still indirectly enjoying the proceeds of slavery passed on to them, according to Dr Draper from the University College London.

After its formal abolition, white slave traders were awarded massive amounts in compensation for the loss of slaves, what is equivalent to modern day Billions of pounds. That is how many of today's rich white families maintain their lavish lifestyle and inherit industries and institutions.

Among those revealed to have benefited from slavery include the ancestors of the UK's previous Tory Prime Minister, David Cameron.

The same Prime Minister that pledged to spend £25 million on building a prison in Jamaica, so that Jamaican nationals locked up in the UK can be sent home to Jamaica to serve sentences there.

Ex Prime Minister David Cameron announced the deal as he began a visit to Jamaica in 2015. However, the Jamaican Prime Minister, Portia Simpson-Miller spoke directly to David Cameron and called for Britain to pay reparations for its role in the slave trade, but Cameron told reporters that financial reparations were "not the right approach". He is willing however, to spend £25 mill on a prison.

Rather than pay for the crimes of Britain's ancestors and help build up one of the countries that it colonised, or invest the money in deprived black council estates in the UK to prevent black males going to prison in the first instance, the UK would rather invest money in negative ventures such as prison.

And similar systems are applied in the United States. The 13th Amendment to the US Constitution abolished slavery and involuntary servitude except as a punishment for crime where people are convicted.

This means once you are convicted of a crime and serving in a prison they have the right to use you as a slave. As I previously explained slavery still exists, just the format of its structure has changed, and you can see how law is used to make exploration and murder acceptable as legal.

The 13th Amendment enables prisons to use people as slaves, they carry out work as though they are employees but they do not get paid. The large corporations that are in bed with the prisons exploit the 13th Amendment and have inmates acting as their employees to make their products and goods for them.

Since the abolition of slavery, black males have continued as commodities transferring from the plantations to the prison economy through the criminal justice system.

The private management of prisons is big money, naturally in a society that has no problem using human commodities there is profit to be gained in prisons.

The prison economic profit is not only gained by the private companies that manage prisons, it is all of the other white-owned businesses and service providers that it takes to run a prison.

The uniforms, the shoes, badges, the food and cooking utensils, the vending machines, maintenance equipment and supply of the office materials, the prisoner education and rehabilitation programmes; added to which are the wardens, secretaries, prison guards who maintain their businesses, middle-class lifestyle, steady employment, retirement pensions, cars, homes all on the mass imprisonment of the black man. Everybody wins economically at the expense of, and the exploitation of the black prisoner.

The UK has outsourced cleaning and maintenance of more than a hundred public sector prisons. Private companies have placed bids for five-year contracts each worth a total of £100m a year. Electronic Tagging of prisoners contracts are worth £44 million for an initial 7 months, with the prospect of a 10 year extension.

Two companies have been put in charge of the Seventy percent of the probation service that has been privatised in England and Wales under the most far-reaching privatisation in the criminal justice system. These contracts are worth approximately £450m.

Please be aware that prison is a business and black people are its biggest asset. As a collective we must work together to prevent ourselves from becoming prison commodities.

Self Investigation

We all know that the criminal justice system is racist, the statistics and evidence speaks for itself. We know that if black males were to suddenly stop going to prison and live a productive family life and build up their communities it wouldn't really serve well for the whole prison economy.

Nonetheless, the UK Government announced in the media, the first week in February 2016, that (Black) Labour Member of Parliament for Tottenham, David Lammy, is to head a new government review into discrimination against black and ethnic minority people in the criminal justice system.

David Cameron said the review would address "possible sentencing and prosecutorial disparity". He added: "If you're black, you're more likely to be in a prison cell than studying at a top university".

"And if you are black it seems you're more likely to be sentenced to custody for a crime than if you're white. We should investigate why this is and how we can end this possible discrimination." He said.

Hmm...White people calling for an investigation to find out if they are being racist towards black people, then they will stop themselves being racist. It's a nonsense!

An investigation into the Criminal Justice System is not required to tell us what we already know. The system is racist and the evidence speaks loud and clear.

Investigations of this type are a waste of time, they will not solve the problem of institutional racism. They are no more than a subterfuge to keep you reliant upon the system and pacify you, to make it appear that racism is being dealt with when in fact it will not and cannot be resolved by its perpetrators.

Remembering Stephen Lawrence

Remember the 1999 Stephen Lawrence inquiry. Stephen Lawrence, the 19 year old boy that dreamed of being an architect had his whole life ahead of him, was murdered in 1999 in cold blood by a group of racist savages.

It took his parents over twenty years to get justice for their son as the system initially allowed the racist savages to walk away from justice scot-free.

The Metropolitan police failed in their investigation procedures due to their racist agent mentality and as a result a public inquiry was ordered into the Metropolitan Police Service handling of the case.

Lord Macpherson undertook the inquiry and found that the police were institutionally racist.

New laws were introduced (civil law) to ensure that the police basically didn't act racist in the exercise of their duties, and police forces as a body could be held to account.

They had a General Duty (legal duty) to: Eliminate unlawful racial discrimination; promote equality of opportunity and; good race relations. The law also applied to other public authorities listed within the schedule of the Act, to include the NHS, Borough Councils, housing associations and other public body organisations.

The law introduced was the Race Relations Act 2000 as amended, known as The Race Equality Duty.

I was working at the Commission for Racial Equality at the time of the induction of the Race Duty, my role was to enforce the Race Duty throughout the London and South of England Region, so I had insight into how the law operated and how it was received by the police and other public bodies who were under a legal obligation to comply with it. It was basically a paper exercise.

We have seen public inquiries and investigations by the State before, it is not new. The Race Duty did not prevent police forces killing young black males, black males were still being sent to jail disproportionately and black males are still dying at the hands of police.

Black youths were still being stopped and searched disproportionately, the police forces were still discriminating against their Black and Asian staff. Nothing changed, racism was still being executed on a daily basis.

Member of Parliament David Lammy's report findings of the investigation into the criminal justice system that "greater disproportionality" in the number of black people in prisons in England and Wales than in the US. Black people make up 3% of population in England and Wales and 12% of the prison population, compared with 13% and 35% respectively, in the US, as well as other negative findings, will not change the plight of the black nation, and that is guaranteed.

Racism is inherent within the system and people are conditioned to execute it. The minds of white people cannot be changed through investigation or laws that they create, you have seen evidence of that.

You can be guaranteed of one thing, no amount of police initiatives, such as Operation Trident and the likes there of, or independent reviews into death in custody by the Secretary of State, Stop and Search 'unconscious bias' training for the police, or investigations into the criminal justice system will eliminate racism, discrimination and the systematic destruction of the black race. They are all a subterfuge. Black people will continue to experience oppression and racism as long as you and I continue to live our lives as integrated parts of the system.

Black Sterling Action Step 2

Chapter one 'who controls the system that controls you' dissected many factors of the system and its negative impacts including education institutions, the criminal justice system and broken homes.

We as black people need to make radical changes in order to keep our people out of the criminal justice system and overall escape the eurocentric controlled systems of oppression and eliminate its negative impacts by creating our own economic systems which is the way forward, however it is a tall order and will take time. In the meantime there are small easy steps that we can take towards realising that reality.

We can align ourselves with organisations that are working with young people and parents to empower them and provide life skills that will steer them away from a life of crime. One such organisation which provides this is called the Manhood Academy that turns boys into men using a Gambian manhood ceremony and community mentoring programmes and transformational workshops. Another such organisation is 100 Black Men of London which also provides community mentoring programmes for young people for boys and girls alike to achieve their potential and become leaders in their community. To get involved in their project you can visit them at: http://www.100bml.org/ and www.manhoodacademy.co.uk

Providing education institutions for our children is a major incentive and an absolute must. Kay Johnston, the founder of The Nubian Ministry of Education is seeking parents and mentors from diverse careers, and businesses whom can offer employment. Contact us via the Black Sterling website and we can put you in touch with Kay Johnston. www.blacksterling.uk or just contact me on Facebook.

AUTHOR'S NOTE

MY STORY IS YOUR STORY

"One cannot ask the people that inflict racism upon them to stop that racism, and give you equality, pride and dignity. It is a foolish notion indeed that we must realise will never come to pass." – Khadijah Ward

My Story is Your Story

Martin Luther King Jr, says we may have come on all different ships but we are all in the same boat now. And that we are. As I said in the introduction, we may have been planted on different Caribbean Islands, but we experience racism and oppression all the same, under the same system.

My story is your story pretty much, like you I am a product of the African Holocaust.

One of my sister's had a DNA test and it revealed that on my mother's side we are Haplogroup L3 only found in Africa, and originating in East Africa more specifically Ethiopia. Our ancestors then migrated to West Africa and from there into slavery. Last stop…dumped on the Caribbean Island of Barbados.

I met both my grandmother and great grandmother at the same time when my mother took me back to Barbados at the age of sixteen. My grandmother was in her 70s and my great-grandmother in her nineties. I am totally gutted that I do not have photos of us together, an opportunity lost unfortunately.

My grandmother died in 2013 at the ripe old age of 110 years old. Even at that age she was a vibrant, outspoken and bossy woman. However she went blind as she refused to have a retina operation that could have saved her sight.

She told me many stories, and I only wish that I had recorded them. I can tell you however that she worked as a maid for white people, so pretty much a life of servitude.

One of my mothers first jobs was picking cotton, and again it was for the white plantation owners. Clearly the money she earned was not life changing, as you don't get rich by working on the plantation, old or modern day. She earned a measly few dollars to help her get by, whilst the plantation owner on the other hand was filthy rich.

I have four sisters and one brother some of us were left behind when my father travelled from Barbados to the UK in 1959 to seek his fortune, he then sent for my mother in 1960. So I grew up without my big brother and my sister who were left behind with a plan to be sent for at a later date but it never happened.

In addition I also have two half-sisters and brother on my father's side. I was very close to my little brother, who incidentally is the image of my father, and I have been in his life since his birth.

I first met my sister Sharon in 2015 when my father was diagnosed with prostate cancer and we became close. I was my father's official carer up until his death, in fact, my older sister Ayesha, and I witnessed him taking his last breath, which at the same time gave me both a heartbreaking and erie feeling.

My father had a plan to make his fortune in Britain and return to Barbados with all the family much better off after ten years. However life has a way of going in the opposite direction to how we plan it, and my father never returned to Barbados to live, he stayed in the UK and died here after fifty-seven years in a foreign land his dream failed to materialise.

I was put through the euro-centric education system because the controllers of the system have passed laws that say that is what we as citizens have to do, so my parents did.

I was an exceptionally bright child, however the system is not designed for people like me, black and bright. I did great on exams and tests and I aced the 11 plus exam so the headmaster advised my parents to send me to a grammar school outside of the borough.

I was in the top class of my secondary school but I was always bored in school. I had absolutely no interest in what I was being taught, it was pure garbage! So I acted out most of the time, played truant and just drifted along. However I loved athletics, netball, English and Art.

'Blackie and Rubber lips'

My form teacher, when I was 11 years old was a psycho bitch called Mrs Chorwill. I remember the name, the hateful personality and the ugly face and awful body shape as though it were yesterday. And even at my young age I was surprised that she was a married woman, after all how could anybody be attracted to that, I thought.

Both my parents were good looking, as were my aunts and uncles so I was used to being surrounded by beauty. And having to go to school and look at Chorwill all day I found offensive to my eyes.

She also taught us for French which I found utterly ridiculous, she had a thick accent which I believe was Scottish, and trying to speak French just sounded wrong, it just came across as stupid.

Anyway Chorwill hated my guts! And I can only put it down to racism. I was in the top class and the only black child in that top class. Chorwill hated me for it and belittled me every chance she could get for no reason. She was a racist thug! Who thought it acceptable to bully an eleven year old child.

Prior to my secondary school experience I remember getting into fights with boys a lot in primary school after being racially abused in the playground being called 'blackie' or 'rubber lips'. I am sure you remember those times?

My father taught my siblings and I how to fight and not to take any abuse from anyone, so I was confident to physically fight when I was racially abused.

I experienced my first racial abuse attack as an adult at the age of 21. I had just dropped my son off at nursery school, in the City and I rushed to the post office opposite the school to buy a stamp before going to work.

It was a Monday, so there was a very long queue. Nevertheless, I joined the queue and moved up the line in order like everybody else, when a scruffy white man aged approximately early sixties tried to push his way in front of me.

I politely challenged him making him aware that he was pushing in, and explained to him that I was before him asking him to take his place at the back.

He must have felt embarrassed that he was being publicly told off by a woman, and a young black woman nonetheless, he then took it upon himself to call me a "f-ing nigger!"

Being bit of a 'hot head' back in the day, I'm afraid I did not contain myself or act with dignity, I saw red and retaliated by saying, "Let me show you what a nigger can do" and proceeded to whack him hard across the face.

I remember hearing a woman in the queue gasp, the man himself turned bright red, he did not strike back I think he may have been too shocked, but he managed to shout out to the post office staff to call the police.

I was no longer in the mood to stand in a queue waiting to buy a stamp, and I was not about to wait for the arrival of the police either to see whether they would take the side of an older white man or that of a young black woman, so at that point I made a swift exit.

After I had time to settle down and think about what had just happened, I could not believe that a grown man had just called me a 'nigger' in broad day light in a very public place.

I had retaliated to the abuse with a slap but that was a reaction. I wondered how I could stop that behaviour being projected towards me in the first place, but I could not reach any solutions.

I was living in a white society, I thought therefore I would encounter white people, and on some rare occasions I would experience overt racism.

I was young and 'green' a product of the system, I was taught to get an education and get a 'good job' so it never occurred to me at the point in my life to try and remove myself from a system where the odds were stacked against me.

Let's call a Spade a Spade

It was 1983 I had no idea where my life was going. I was dealing with the here and now trying to make ends meet as a single parent.

So, I worked part-time on the corporate plantation for Ladbrokes betting offices in Holborn West London, which incidentally was the most mind-numbing job that I have ever had. Dealing with layabouts, and down-and-outs spending their last pennies on gambling trying to get the big win on the horses and dogs.

I was on the payout till, which meant I paid the customers winning bets. At the end of one evening the betting office was robbed and I had to give the robbers, one white and the other black, all the money from the payout till as a gun was being held to the manager's head — they escaped on a motorbike.

Incidentally, I remember having extreme difficulty getting my car insured when I informed insurers that I worked for a bookie, as back in the 80s bookies were being robbed regularly, so insurers saw working for them as high risk.

When the police arrived on the scene my colleagues and I gave an account of events and I described the robbers. The police officer radioed in the descriptions, and this so called officer of the law felt absolutely no way that I was sitting right next to him, and as cool and calm as ever, as though he was talking about going to the shop to buy a loaf of bread, proceeded to describe the black male robber as a "Spade." His comfortable and audacious attitude demonstrates that describing black people as spades was clearly common practice amongst police forces.

In the introduction we discussed how the word black is used as a negative connotation, day after day as a part of the system and is accepted as normal behaviour.

The behaviour of the police officer at Ladbrokes premises demonstrated to me that racism is executed as normal and acceptable behaviour by those within the western power structure to subjugate and oppress black people, and to make us feel bad about our skin colour.

He didn't make me feel bad about my skin colour, he just made me feel angry that I had to sit and listen to a derogatory comment made about one of my people, robber or not, and there was nothing that I could actually do about it.

As one gets older one realises that physical attacks are not the way to deal with racism. Even though there is instant gratification upon giving "Johnny" one lick inna 'im 'ead for verbally abusing you, they are reactive measures, and reactive measures, in my experience do not solve ingrained issues of an age old problem such as racism.

Dealing with systemic racism requires strategy. A collective, organised and sophisticated approach which is what this book is all about.

Working inside the System

Well, the racism followed me from the playground to the corporate plantation. In more or less every corporation I have worked for I have experienced racial discrimination, not covert racial abuse, but overt systemic racial discrimination.

I was taught as a child to work on the corporate plantation, so I did so, blindly without question. There came a point in my life when I recognised that the system was indeed racist, and I thought that I could try to change things from the inside.

I spent two decades as a leading authority in race relations and as a professional dealing with anti-discrimination law and human rights. Enforcing the law against public authorities and also advocating for the 'little man' with his or her complaints of discrimination. Fighting against injustice foolishly trying to change the behaviours of those within the corporate plantation.

I managed to reach director level in particular corporations, which the system allowed me to do, however, I was eventually brought down by the very racism that I was trying to counteract.

Nobody called me a 'nigger' or 'blackie,' nothing as overt as that, but it was thought that as a black person I was earning far too much money, raising too many issues, and welding too much authority, therefore I needed to be reminded of 'my place'.

So surprise, surprise I was brought down through the system. On one occasion by an old hag munchkin of a woman. I was told by others that she was jealous of me, I was earning more much more than her and my annual bonus was 20% hers was 5%. I was more popular than her and intellectually superior. The envy must have been too much, so by sexing the overseers and whispering sweet poison in their ears she got me ousted.

Suspension, disciplinary and redundancy were three of the corporate plantation whips that were used to bring me down. I am sure that many of you can resonate with my plight.

Trying to change the minds and behaviours of people cannot be done by working within a system entrenched with racism, it is virtually impossible. And complaining about it is also a complete waste of time.

My time of working on the plantation was up. I decided to take my power back by never putting myself at their mercy again.

I have removed myself from the euro-centric oppressive system to achieve self-reliance as far as possible as an individual is able to. I no longer work on a corporate plantation I run my own business and have achieved financial independence.

I don't live on a government council run estate, I own two properties so I don't have to worry about being oppressed by government housing policies although I do worry about my brothers and sisters that find themselves at the mercy of the draconian housing laws and policies.

I buy black! Supporting my brothers and sisters in the purchase of their products, goods and services as a priority regardless of cost. For whatever I need I always check if a black-owned store has it first. If a store that is near to me sells products I want and it is not black-owned I wont purchase from them I seek out a black-owned business to make my purchase.

However, being self-reliant as an individual wont create a black economic system I need unity with you my brothers and sisters in order to achieve a community of collective economic independence and power.

Believe me our life as black people can be better, and I am counting on you to work with me to invest in the future of our community. At the end of the book you will be directed on how we can work together to build a brighter future for us all.

Racial discrimination law is a farce

There are laws in place that enable people to make claims against their employer for racial discrimination, or service providers.

In the workplace you can lodge a grievance of discrimination, take the matter before an employment tribunal. We follow a process when we are racially discriminated against in the workplace, but to achieve what outcome?

When you lodge internal grievances the findings are always that no discrimination has occurred anyway. Corporate plantations will never admit to discrimination.

The internal grievance and employment tribunal processes that you follow in order to eliminate racism are reactive measures that truly have no real positive outcomes, they are of no consequence, and do not change the quality of your life or that of the black community as a whole.

Once you make allegations of racial discrimination in the plantation, the working environment will become even worse making it difficult for you to remain in employ. So you leave and hope that the next plantation that you join treats you better than the last.

After you have gone through the process, does your life actually change for the better, or does it positively impact that of your fellow black brothers and sisters? The answer is that it does not.

This is a system of white people making findings against other white people, of course they wont find for discrimination. You proceed to an employment tribunal, and on occasions the tribunal will find in your favour but not often.

Last year the average award at employment tribunal for a complaint of racial discrimination was £6000, hardly bloody worth all the stress.

I made a complaint of racial discrimination and unfair dismissal against my employers in 1998, I took it to Tribunal and represented myself. I won and was paid out £5000. It was great at the time, I ran out and purchased a pair of boots that I had my eye on, however in the long run, the bigger picture it served no purpose whatsoever.

Racism is Here to Stay

I was still discriminated against in my future employment on the corporate plantation, and it did not do anything to further the cause of my brothers and sisters either.

Despite the anti-discrimination laws in place, racism is practiced every day. Black people still undergo racist treatment on a daily basis in all aspects of society, since the arrival of our parents in the 1950s and 60s.

Remember, the laws upon which we rely to obtain redress for racism and discrimination, are laws developed and passed by white law makers of the power structure. They have the control, so they develop and pass laws and can apply any restrictions that they see fit. They are creator, judge and jury.

Do not be fooled into thinking that because we have laws that enable us to undertake a process of redress we have progress, they are a smoke screen of distraction to give the illusion of progression.

In one hand they give you a process of redress, whilst on the other, if you dare to use the process for claims of racial discrimination against your employer, your employer will victimise you. Another bullying tactic when you make complaints is you're 'pulling the race card'

Under the current anti-discrimination laws racism and racial discrimination is prohibited. A judicial process exists for redress to challenge alleged discriminatory treatment. But race discrimination is hard to prove and it can sometimes be a very emotionally taxing and time consuming process for people.

In any event, it does not change a thing, least of all the lives of the black masses under sufferance.

Poem - Beware, the deadly Smiling Assassin

A poem for you about the system to whet your appetite, enjoy...

He smiles as in one hand he gives you seeds of hope, he smiles in the other you get an ounce of dope.

He smiles when he grants you race relations law, he smiles, when his racism makes you stay poor.

He smiles, as he lets you integrate his schools, he smiles, as education turns you his fool.

He smiles as you spit your profanity rap, he smiles as young brothers kill each other, cap! Cap!

He smiles when you make a career out of crime, he smiles when his judge says, now do whole heap of time.

He smiles as you form your 'hood' street gang, he smiles as his police guns dem bang! Bang!

The smiling assassin is a deadly machine, a force to be reckoned like a guillotine, beware, as he smiles he wipes you out clean, your Black liberation becomes a pipe-dream. End of poem.

This poem provides you with an insight of how you are manipulated by the system.

I worked for the Commission for Racial Equality for six years, the UK non-departmental government legislative body, set up under the Race Relations Act 1976, to execute legislation around race relations, its mission was to; eliminate unlawful race discrimination and promote equality of opportunity.

It had 90% Black and Asian staff, The Chairman was Black, succeeded by an Asian Chairman. Heck, my first manager was black, Anthony Robinson, and the director thereafter was also black. It was a great place to work because I was surrounded by like-minded people.

But alas, even though there was a high number of black staff in authority we were agents of the government. The Commission was a government controlled body which meant that it had to operate within the system and answer to the UK government, the Home Office, therefore the power of the black leaders were limited and controlled.

Eventually just like all race issues the Commission for Racial Equality became a nuisance to the power structure so it was taken out of the hands of Black and Asian people under the pretext of a merger of all other equality commissions bringing the law as one piece of legislation.

The new body, the Equality & Human Rights Commission, under a uniformed piece of legislation was placed in the hands of white people.

The Equality and Human Rights Commission, or the EHRC as it is commonly known is a predominately white organisation where race issues are a thing of the past, buried along with the body that once championed it.

You see, where the white power structure is in control, it can do exactly as it pleases, and we as black people are at the mercy of it. If they are fed up with playing around with race issues, or race issues are becoming too prominent or complicated, then they will shut it down! Simple! They make the laws, they control how it operates.

It happens in all areas of the corporate world which you as black people strive so hard to be a part of. If you manage to rise, they will drag you down at the drop of a hat. If you speak out about injustice, rest assured you will be taken out!

Remember the poem, "They grant you race relations law while racism keeps you poor". The laws that are passed to 'protect' you only to a certain point.

The Equality Act 2010 will not Stop Systemic Racism

Prior to the induction of the Race Relation Act 1976 and the current Equality Act 2010 black people could be told straight to their face you are not being hired for a job because you are black, or I am not renting you my property because you are black.

Now that the laws are in place, the only difference is, is that people will not tell you direct to your face. However people that want to perpetrate racism will do so, despite any laws that are in place. They do not fear the laws.

In 2009 the UK Government's Department of Work and Pensions undertook research as undercover job hunters and revealed huge race bias in Britain's workplaces. Civil servants created false identities to send CVs to hundreds of employers in a sting to uncover discrimination.

Researchers sent nearly 3,000 job applications under false identities in an attempt to discover if employers were discriminating against job-seekers with foreign names.

Using names recognisably from three different communities – Nazia Mahmood, Mariam Namagembe and Alison Taylor – false identities were created with similar experience and qualifications. Every false applicant had British education and work histories.

They found that an applicant who appeared to be white would send nine applications before receiving a positive response of either an invitation to an interview or an encouraging telephone call. African and Asian candidates with the same qualifications and experience had to send 16 applications before receiving a similar response.

The report concludes that there was no plausible explanation for the difference in treatment found between white British and ethnic minority applicants other than racial discrimination.

These research exercises are all well and good but they do not change anything. Racial discrimination in recruitment will always exist, despite equal opportunities and anti-discrimination legislation. Law will not stop the racism.

The token gestures of power given to people placed in authority such as Judges, police officers and magistrates will not have actual power to significantly change anything for the black community as a whole.

We have seen the legislative protection we have been given, and tokens in positions of authority, that give the illusion that our lives are better, but it wont bring about real economic wealth, justice and equality for your community.

After 400 years of slavery you are still being treated like slaves, and you continue to fall for the trappings of the system, believing that your oppressors will stop oppressing you.

Remember, the system allowed you to be there, therefore you have to work within its rules and regulations if you want to stay within it.

How much more convincing do you actually need to see that this system does not work in your favour and it never will.

You must be aware that there is a problem with this current system, that shows a pattern in the destruction of the black race. Black people need not require any more evidence than there already is to realise that integration within the white infrastructure has failed you.

You have seen and lived how the euro-centric education and criminal justice systems operate, and the devastating effects that these systems have on you and your young people. You remain poor, dysfunctional and are dying prematurely, at the hands of the State.

Yet you have come to accept the system and all the negativities that it brings as a way of life, without giving consideration to possible alternatives.

Shouldn't you stop begging and relying upon the corporate plantation to give you jobs, equality and dignity? Wouldn't it make more sense to try and remove yourselves from it as far as possible and become self-reliant as a community?

In the interest of the survival and prosperity of the black race, you cannot continue to accept a system in which you are systematically oppressed, that will see your ultimate destruction.

One Woman's Story of Self-Reliance

My younger sister removed herself from the system of racism at the age of twenty-four. She worked for a Bank and left because she hated the system. It was her only job working on the corporation plantation and she decided to take up a profession where she need not rely on the system, where she could be her own boss, independent and in control.

She became an entrepreneur and created her own driving school, which she has had for the past twenty-three years.

She supports black-owned businesses by purchasing their products and services first and foremost. Ever since starting her business she commissioned African printers for her business cards via the then, 1990s UK 'Black Pages.'

She has no negative interaction with law enforcement or courts. She experiences no racism because she is self-reliant and lives independent of the system as much as she is able to without the structure of a black economic system.

She is co-existing with white people, because Britain is a white country, and some white people are her customers, but that is fine because they hold no power over her as she is not economically reliant upon them.

The 2011 census showed 1,904,684 declared themselves as Black British, that is not including people that declared themselves as Black African or Caribbean.

Imagine if we multiplied the above woman's story of self-reliance and entrepreneurship, and times it by twenty percent of the census number of the UK Black British population statistics, we could create our own economic infrastructure. Black people buying each others products and services, Black people owning their own businesses, Black people building industries within Black communities.

Black Sterling Action Step 3

Aspire to become an entrepreneur, or work for black-owned organisations. Stop making white companies rich and remove your self from the racist corporate plantation.

I have shared some of my stories of racism on the corporate plantation with you and I have no doubt that you can resonate with them, you may also have worse stories than I.

We have seen the impact of black people working in the white corporate structure. We not only face racism and racial discrimination on a daily basis in these structures but we are helping to make white corporations rich and maintain poverty in the black community.

Rich white corporations mean rich white communities, so surely rich black corporations should equal rich black communities, right. If we create them that is. There are too many talented black people out there whose talents would be better served in the black community.

We need to create jobs for people of the black community to help you run your business. In-turn we need to commission fellow black-owned businesses as suppliers of goods and services for your companies.

You also heard how my sister escaped the corporate plantation after round one and chose to become an entrepreneur 'one woman's story of self-reliance'. It is about choices, we can make choices now that we are no longer legal commodities of the State so you should make the right ones that help us all build a community.

I escaped the oppressive euro-centric system of the corporate plantation and I feel much freer and better for it. All it takes is an idea, courage, will power and support from your people. Then you have to take steps to realise the idea into entrepreneur status. Of course it takes hard work, success is always hard work, but the end result and the feelings of independence are second to none.

Now I am asking you my people to join me to work together to create a brighter future for us and our next generation.

Still in chains, read on…

CHAPTER THREE

STILL IN CHAINS

"Who taught you to hate yourself? Who taught you to hate the texture of your hair? Who taught you to hate the colour of your skin? To such extent you bleach, to get like the white man. Who taught you to hate the shape of your nose and the shape of your lips? Who taught you to hate yourself from the top of your head to the soles of your feet? Who taught you to hate your own kind? Who taught you to hate the race that you belong to so much so that you don't want to be around each other? No... Before you come asking Mr. Muhammad does he teach hate, you should ask yourself who taught you to hate being what God made you." —MalcolmX

Slave mentality is a significant discussion point. The reason being, it's a major hindrance in black progression. We are our own worst enemy as many of us still think like slaves.

You may be familiar with one of Malcolm X's speeches, "Who taught you to hate yourself." The speech goes on to say, "Who taught you to hate the texture of your hair"

Who taught you to hate the colour of your skin to such extent, that you bleach to get like the white man?

Who taught you to hate the shape of your nose and the shape of your lips. Who taught you to hate yourself from the top of your head to the soles of your feet?

Who taught you to hate your own kind? Who taught you to hate the race that you belong to so much so that you don't want to be around each other?"

Malcolm X's main message was that the African Holocaust, and current day racism led many black people to despise themselves.

"The worst crime the white man has committed, he said, has been to teach us to hate ourselves. Self-hatred caused Black Americans to lose their identity, straighten their hair, and become involved in crime, drug addiction, and alcoholism."

The words of Malcolm X are sad, but true. Due to the African Holocaust, the indoctrination of slaves and its legacy, the black man subconsciously hates himself.

He acts as though he has no recollection of his previous ruling nations, true history and nobility with no belief in his own self-worth or abilities. How come? And to what consequence?

The 'How Come'

The African Holocaust stole our history, our education, our wealth, our native languages, our names, our customs, culture, beliefs and all that belonged to us. Fact!

Including our dignity, self-worth, self reliance, and the ability to think for ourselves, as organised leaders, trans-atlantic traders and builders of industries wealth and communities.

If nothing else, the legacy of the African Holocaust should teach you that the black mans self-hate was indoctrinated through a system of white oppressive supremacy.

By means of 400 years of inhuman treatment, enslavement, lynching, torture, rape, castration, brain-washing, punishment, penalty and genocide, an evil beyond belief of any normal human being's comprehension.

Many of us believe, our younger generation in particular, that as black people we were living like jungle animals before Europeans enslaved us, due to the portrayal of Africans as savages and 'jungle bunnies' and the colour black as a negative which also keeps us conditioned after our emancipation.

We believe that the white man is superior, so everything that he sees as worthless, we see as worthless. What he holds in high regard we also hold in high regard.

His way of life, and his beliefs are king in our minds, and our only means of survival are through his systems and his hand-outs.

There remains a reliance and dependency for the black mans basic human needs upon the Europeans through his systems and customs. We strive for his acceptance, respect and equal treatment that places us at the mercy of the Eurocentric system.

Even after the legal abolition of the slave trade, though it pains me to say, black people are still very much modern day slaves.

The subconscious feeling of self-hate, unworthiness and inferiority to the white man is woven through the very fabric and existence of the black man today as we exhibit many self-destructive behaviours.

Some black people, and I would say a high percentage of us, are unaware of the full extent to which they are conditioned under this racist system. Our child-like display for dependency, respect and acceptance is evident to the degree that we are advocates of the system that oppresses us without even realising it.

We merrily adopt the slave masters descendent's customs as our own, that is the extent of the systems sophistication. We have never really recovered from the impact of the systematic atrocities bestowed upon us.

The Consequence of Slavery

The African Holocaust is clearly the reason that you are bound to a fate of the oppressive system that controls you. You were taught self-hate and dependency and now find it hard to escape.

In fact, many of us do not want to escape, as we are unaware that we are even in a deep-rooted state of hypnosis and control.

For example, we deny the uniqueness of our hair and try to make it look like Europeans. Hair straightening, we have all been guilty of it, I will be the first to hold my hands up.

Hair straightening is a multi-billion pound industry, so clearly many of us are straightening our hair. This is not a judgement upon anyone, this is a statement of fact, and awareness raising, of how slavery has made black people deny the very characteristics that make us unique.

Prior to slavery, the black woman's hair was pride and joy. She would adorn various natural hairstyles, including plaiting and extension plaiting.

However, when African people were captured as slaves, the hair was initially cut off, and we were made to cover our hair with raps. Thereafter, the hair was something not to be proud but to hide.

Simply put, we were made to hate the texture and look of our hair, which was a major step towards eradicating the African identity.

Skin Lightening

Another form of slave mentality, is skin-bleaching. The act of a black person using skin creams that lighten the skin, is clear evidence that one does not like the original colour of their skin, and or the lighter skin-tone is deemed to be better.

Your ancestors were taught during slavery that your skin colour represented all that was bad and worthless therefore we try to adopt a skin-tone that brings us nearer to looking like our oppressors. There is no other explanation for our skin-lightening practices.

Your ancestors were taught to hate their facial features and everything about themselves, and that self-hate is passed down and projected upon others that look like them. The famous Jackson family for example, every one of them changed their wide nose through surgery, now that is not an act of liking your nose that is an act of disliking it.

Even our attire is western. We were stripped of our heritage and customs and today, African Caribbean people wear western clothes. We all do, we are used to wearing clothes of a culture that does not belong to us through conditioning and control. These are some of the consequences of the traumatic legacy of being enslaved.

Your Nubian Queen - Love Her she's Precious

"The Black man will never get any respect until he respects his own women."—Malcolm X

Yes, another Malcolm X quote, sorry but I have to keep quoting him, because that man was just genius! If black people of today were to follow his teachings we would find ourselves in a place of self-love realisation and united economic power.

One of the most dangerous outcomes of the slave trade's indoctrination of the black man, is his obsession with the white man's ideal of beauty. The white man continues to denigrate the black man as a race yet still he chases after their ideals.

We do not see other races of men obsessing and taking preference on a grand scale over another race's woman because they have not experienced the indoctrination of self-hate of centuries, in fact, the white woman, is portrayed by the white man as the ultimate ideal of beauty and is elevated on a pedestal, and there is nothing wrong with that, in fact that is what he should be doing it is his woman.

The black man should also do the same with his woman, however a vast majority do not. A high percentage of black men do not see the the beautiful black as an extension of himself. He sees what the white man sees, and he craves the indoctrinated image of the slave masters considered best above his own because his mind has been twisted for four hundred years and the legacy continues.

In my mind the physical comparisons between a black woman and white woman considered, well, a black woman wins hands down. Black woman have a beautiful skin colour, extremely full lips, tight body with a full round buttocks, beautiful muscular yet feminine bodies. Just to name a few of the exceptional physical attributes.

Despite the visual beautiful attributes of the black woman, she is perceived to be the most unattractive and disrespected woman on the planet, even by her own black men. And if your own men do not see you as beautiful how can one expect the rest of the world.

I have witnessed video interviews where black boys as young as fifteen years old speak of their preference for all other woman apart from their own black woman. It made me feel quite sad to see that the black woman is seen as a nothing, the bottom of the pile of all other women by these young and impressionable young men whom have black mothers and sisters and will be the leaders of tomorrow's nation.

From the presenters of the Kiss FM Takeaway show, to films such as Kidulthood. And jack arses' like Ice T, publicly declaring 'ten reasons why black men prefer white woman.' Incidentally, is Ice T a Black man though, hmm...the jury is still out on that one.

Where does that leave black women? When the ratio of women to men is higher to begin with, and then you are left with at least 60% of the males of the race going elsewhere. The future looks bleak.

The black nation cannot unite and build a black economy without the black man. He is the leader and strength of the race therefore he must take the reins in order to bring about black liberation.

Black men, must first and foremost love the black woman, she must be his first choice. She is beautiful and precious, her beauty and physical attributes are second to none. She is the reason for your very being, she is your mother, your sister, the one that shares your history and your plight, she identifies with you, and she produces children in your image.

Do not be brainwashed or fooled into thinking that other women are better than your own black women, that is slave mentality taking hold.

Black men, you must not verbally attack the black woman with harsh comments about character and hair, these are just excuses and justifications for your own behaviour. You are disrespecting yourself.

Publicly elevating the white woman and putting down the black woman is the behaviour of a buffoon, please stop it, you are embarrassing yourself. These are reasons that no other race respects the black man because he does not respect himself.

In the words of Malcolm X "The Black man will never get any respect until he respects his own women."

This is not slavery of old where the black man was not able to protect his woman because he had no power. He was stripped of his masculinity and had to stand by and watch the denigration of the black woman. You are now in a position to protect and stand by the black woman and you must do so.

What's in a Name?

Even today, after four generations through continued training and habit, we still wear the slave masters names.

Remember the Alex Haley film 'Roots'. The main character Kunta Kinte was based on one of his ancestors, a Gambian man who was born in 1750, enslaved and taken to America.

The Kunta Kinte character in the film was 'whooped' until he denounced his African name and declared his name as Toby, the name given to him by the slave master.

Once upon a time I owned a dog, a Rottweiler, and I named him Sultun. Sultun did not have a say in what I named him, he lacked the capacity to argue or reason and I as his master was in control, therefore what I said would be. Simple! Your name is Sultun and you must answer to it and he did.

The same principle applied to African people during slavery, the ability to have a say in what your ancestors or their children were called was taken away.

We were not allowed to have our African names, we were named like masters would name a dog, and so we named our children European names and continue to do so in the present day.

Some may be thinking what's in a name? It shouldn't make any difference what we are called, but it does make a difference. Having European names demonstrates that we have let not go of the African Holocaust legacies.

We are no longer slaves, therefore we should make a conscious effort not to act like slaves in the legal sense of the word. We have choices regarding our names, people can no longer 'whoop' us until we denounce the name of Kunta Kinte and accept the name of 'Toby' which incidentally is a dogs name.

So why would we want to be called names that are a symbolic of our enslavement, unless we are somehow still mentally tied to that enslavement.

If our ancestors were prepared to endure severe pain to try and keep a part of their identity, now that we have choices we should try and denounce slave names as a sign of respect for our ancestors pain, suffering and sacrifice. And, in recognition of who we really are.

Experience has taught me the difference in treatment from white people when you have a European name and a non-European name. With a European name, white people feel more comfortable around you, even though you will still probably experience racism.

Some years ago as a consultant, I was marketing a training product that I developed to white corporations. I told a business man my name, he seemed somewhat taken aback by my name (I ditched my slave name over 25 years ago), and he said that we, (meaning white people) were used to names like Susan and John.

He advised me that upon hearing my name that it may put corporations off from purchasing my services. This is where I need to put an image of an opened mouthed emoji and say WTF!!!

Remember this is a white person telling me how white people think and behave from a white perspective. White people tend to be uncomfortable with non-European names and what the names represent.

They cannot identify with them and do not want to tolerate having to try and pronounce them. They get tongue-tied in the pronunciation, they find it hard to relate to, and sometimes even decide to give you an alternative name that is comfortable and easier for them.

Cassius Clay or Muhammed Ali

The boxer Muhammed Ali, experienced the very same thing. He was previously Cassius Clay, at the age of 22 he won the heavy weight champion of the world title and shortly thereafter he reverted to Islam and became Mohammed Ali.

People in press, including the New York Times refused to refer to Ali by his new name. That is the type of disrespect black people are shown when they try to let go of slavery legacies in something as simple as a name change.

Black people with European names is a demonstration that we hold their customs and behaviour in high regard. The action of adopting another's customs and behaviours as your own is the highest form of flattery and compliment that there is, and also a surrender of your own power.

Imagine if there was a mass changing of names by black people, what a radical message that would send? Think about it. Again, I do not expect everyone to run out and change their name, but such actions carry a lot of weight and create a sense of collective solidarity.

All of the issues identified above, the changing of hair texture, the skin-bleaching, the european names, and all of the other issues are symbolic of continued slave-mentality.

It is this state of mind that makes us subconsciously hate ourselves and anyone that looks like us. Because of this, we fail to unify, organise and work collectively to build empires and undertake the simple task of supporting black-owned businesses as customers or investors. That said, it is time to take action to remove the mental chains and rid yourself of the slave mentality.

The Integration Illusion

"Integration is wrong. We don't want to live with the white man; that's all." —Mohammed Ali

Yes, I keep referring to Mohammed Ali, simply because there are so many examples of how he can be used as an inspiration I would be doing an injustice not to bring them to the forefront of your mind.

In his youth, Mohammed Ali's faith and anger at American racism made him a controversial figure, speaking out against white Americans. He also made open statements that integration does not work for black people.

"Why don't we get out and build our own nation? White people just don't want their slaves to be free. That's the whole thing. Why not let us go and build ourselves a nation? We want a country. We're 40 million people, but we'll never be free until we own our own land." He said.

The late Dick Gregory, social activist, said, "Ali was black and proud of it at a time when many black Americans were running from their colour. He lived a lot of lives for a lot of people, And he was able to tell white folks, for us, to "Go to hell."

The establishment media, and sportswriters in particular came down hard on Ali. Jim Murray of the Los Angeles Times labelled him the 'white man's burden'. However he is no longer a burden, he has been silenced.

Integration is just another form of slavery for black people, we are trained to believe we cannot survive. We fight for acceptance and integration in white corporations.

Many of us argue and campaign for integration because that is all we know, and all that we have been taught. We beg for equality in treatment, diversity in the workplace and acceptance from the people who control the power structure.

I have been guilty of such behaviours, having been brainwashed as a child and trained to study in the euro-centric school system and 'get a good job'.

What has integration done for your race as a whole? It has allowed you to apply for jobs and work within the corporate plantation, and I use the word allowed because it is a system that controls therefore any allowances are given within its control.

It has allowed you laws of redress in equality and race relations, even though we still experience racism every day.

It has allowed some of us individual wealth, riches and a stable lifestyle, but to who's benefit? Only a handful of individuals, a small percentage of the black population benefit.

Even with these hand-outs of integration we do not collectively own anything. Black people are still collectively poor as a race. You do not own industries, or you do not control your own communities.

Black people that were planted on the Caribbean Islands have not had the luxury of large financial inheritances to help set us up on the road to success.

We are not members of 'elite' clubs that enable our children to be educated in fancy schools, or that enable us to walk into investment banking job offers, or given lump sums of money to go off and start a company.

No, the integration of the black man only goes so far in this system and that does not include the 'elite' white clubs that pave the easy road to financial freedom and success.

The majority of black people live in ghettos, young men are involved in gang warfare, men are being locked up, women are raising children alone, and men are being killed in interactions with the police. There are too many negatives as a result of this integrated system.

Don't Beg for Integration

Some time last year there was a plea to the organisation Apple for more diversity in their organisation. Apple's mostly white board's response to the call for diversity was diversity is "unduly burdensome and not necessary." Apple's board of directors recommended that investors vote against a proposal to increase the diversity of its board and senior management.

My response is as follows. So be it. Apple is a white corporation, it is to be expected that they prefer to hire their own. Black people should not be begging Apple for jobs. Heck we could start our own Apple, it was after all a black man that invented the mobile phone forty years ago, Dr. Henry T. Sampson.

Ask yourself, if you manage to get into those media positions what then? A few token black people are given jobs. What power will you have to hire a team of black media specialists? Whose messages will you be portraying in the white institution of media?

It is a Eurocentric media system that uses only white people as models of humanity, and demonises black people with propaganda fuelling hysteria about the "inherent" nature of black criminality and lawlessness.

A few token black people will not have the power to portray positive images of black people in the media, because that would upset the design of the system, and the systems purpose.

The real question is why? Why would black people campaign for integration? The answer to why we would campaign for integration was answered in the chapter three 'still in chains.' Slave mentality, and integration will not help liberate and create collective wealth for the black community.

You cannot look to white people for equality. You cannot look to white people to free black people from racism. Period! It is a ludicrous expectation for black people to expect white people to elevate them to the same status as him.

Imagine this, you know how I like asking you to imagine. You are a billionaire of major corporations, you ride in private jets and have a rich and powerful lifestyle.

You have so much money that you hire a maid called Joanne to clean the toilet, sweep the floor, clean up after you and cook for you etcetera.

Then one day the law changes all maids who have been working for you for twenty years now have to be treated as your equal.

They are entitled to ride next to you in your private jet? Be included in your board meetings. They can attend the Opera with you, sit in your private box and have a financial share in your company.

You would be like, yesterday you were cleaning my toilet now I must share my wealth with you. Regardless of what the law says you still see Joanne the maid as the cleaner of the toilet, you will not see her as equal status to you, and you would not want to give her your wealth or status.

That is how white people see it. We were their slaves, now they are expected to share their wealth with us. Not going to happen. In any event we should not be begging for a piece of the action through integration.

Black Sterling Action Step 4

Rid Yourself of Slave Mentality - Don't Beg for Power. Take It: What Europeans did to us is in the African Holocaust is an unforgivable evil beyond the comprehension of any normal human being. To-date we have not received an apology or one single penny in financial compensation and we cannot sit around waiting for it. What we have received however, is the European's continuous hatred, racism and contempt for us displayed in their behaviour towards us through their structures, systems and politics.

But our slave mentality makes us our own worst enemy, we advocate the system without even realising it, and we cannot progress until we make a conscious effort to drop it and take back our dignity and power.

Equality cannot be given to us either by integration or equality laws, we have to create our competitive advantage and equality ourselves. In chapter one, you were given a solution of how you could contribute to your own self-reliance and that of your nation, and provided with evidence that integration does not work for the Black nation.

The answer to progression is a self-reliant nation. You should not continuously bang on the door for a piece of the action of someplace that does not want you and is of no benefit to you or your community. The answer is not to call for more diversity in industries or for equal opportunity. The answer is get your own!

Integration has failed and will continue to fail you as a Black person, you cannot beat an age old racist system that is set up to destroy you.

Even if some of you manage to infiltrate the system and 'make it big' you are just handfuls of people out of a massive nation. You 'making it big' in the white power structure is at the cost of your own dignity and that of your nation. You are alone working within his system, his rules and his regulations.

For those of you starting out, or if you are already in the music industry, rap conscious lyrics and start a revolution of conscious Black youth. Don't succumb to the slave mentality that makes you sell out and denigrate your race with harmful lyrics in order to profit.

Those of you in the media spotlight, look to Muhammed Ali as an inspiration to follow and take your freedom, dignity and equality.

Those of you ordinary folk, try to wake up and smell the roses! And rid yourselves of slave mentality. Even with an abominable part-history of enslavement and post-slavery endurance of living under terrorist and racist systems, your natural greatness can prevail.

Once upon a time we were rich, read on…

CHAPTER 4

ONCE UPON A TIME WE WERE RICH

Don't Get it Twisted - Ancient Egyptians were Black Africans

Importantly, the issue of ancient Egyptians has to be addressed, as it is a civilisation that is mostly spoken about in the West. And one of which they do not attribute to its rightful owners, black people. It is a rich stolen legacy that must be reclaimed.

Ancient Egypt, was a black African civilisation that euro-centric media like to portray as though it was somehow created by aliens from out of space, Arabs, or white people, anyone but a black African civilisation.

Black Man ('Kemetu') is the original Human, and from where all other Humans descend. Despite popular belief and propaganda, the truth is the black race has created ancient civilisations that have never been replicated.

One of the oldest, ancient Egypt, is one such civilisation. Dating back at least more than 4,000 years B.C.E. and some even suggest more than 10,000 B.C.E.

Scientific studies of DNA have demonstrated that all of modern humanity trace their ancestral roots back to Africa and that Africans are the world's original people. However, it should also be made absolutely clear to the world and black people themselves, that black Africans were not just the world's first human inhabitants, but were also responsible for creating, nurturing and sustaining the world's most highly developed, enduring and arguably technically superior civilisations as well.

Ancient Egyptians referred to themselves as 'Kemetu' translated as Black people. Kemet is the Original Name of Egypt. Egypt or Kemet (its true and original name) is located in the northern part of the continent of Africa, and it is one of Africa's Nile Valley civilisations along with its more southern parent known in ancient times by the Greeks as Nubia (located partly in southern Egypt and partly northern Sudan).

Egypt, like Nubia, was originally inhabited by a purely Black African population similar in look as any other African found in the interior of the continent today. These Africans, our ancestors, were responsible for building the pyramids and temples, the writing, spirituality, high science and culture that Egypt is famed for in our present day.

Ancient Egyptians (Black people) are responsible for providing the world with reading and writing, mathematics, religion, philosophy, art and science. We produced staggering superhuman-like architecture such as the pyramids and temples that both mesmerises and baffles the modern beholder, and quite simply cannot be reproduced even today.

Egypt is so extraordinary that it has the exceptional honour of being the only country that is the subject of scientific study in the form of Egyptology because its superiority of inventions, surgery cannot be matched.

It is not surprising that this captivating and awe-inspiring civilisation has amassed so much attention over the years. It is also not surprising that some groups and races try to claim the Egyptian heritage as their own. (Reference: Journey to the Source.)

A Stolen Legacy

Professor Manu Ampim's research show us that the widespread damage to the temple images has allowed Egyptologists to argue from such sources as the temple evidence that ancient Egypt was a multiracial society and therefore belongs to the world's heritage and not necessarily to African history.

There are probably about a million tourists each year who visit Egypt and Nubia, and they get a totally false view of the identity of the builders of these great civilisations, largely because the evidence of the builders' black origin is disappearing.

This vanishing evidence has enabled dishonest egyptologists and tour guides to misrepresent the identity of the founders and builders of ancient Egypt by selectively pointing out the "non-African" images on the walls. Actually, the images which appear to look "non-African" have undergone a racial make-over and look nothing like they did originally.

These images have been crudely re-carved by European and Arab conspirators who work hard to eliminate all traces of African facial features. Only through exhaustive first-hand research can one demonstrate from the surviving on-site temple evidence that ancient Egypt was indeed a black civilisation.

The altering of black (African) facial features and the lightening of the skin colours of painted reliefs inside the tombs are central aspects of the conspiracy to destroy the memory of classical African civilisations. The two main conspirator groups carrying out these acts are European and American research teams, and local government workers. Throughout Egypt and Nubia, the tomb images have suffered different levels of decay and destruction.

In places such as Giza the tombs are closed as there is little left to see; in Tell Amarna the tomb carvings are in an advanced state of decay; in El Kab and Aswan many of the images have been systematically defaced; and in Beni Hassan only 4 of the 39 tombs are open because the rest are badly damaged. The only major location which has escaped serious tomb damage is Sakkara, but this may not remain true in the future because the conspirators' work is not complete, until they have destroyed or defaced all the evidence of classical African civilisations.

The problem of deterioration of the Kings Valley tombs has led to a growing international movement to build replica tombs and close the original structures. The tomb replication project will likely be implemented in the future. Under this plan, the popular tombs which have suffered irreparable damage, such as the tomb of Tutankhamen, will be permanently closed to the public. Once they are closed, the only persons who will have access to the original Kings Valley tombs will be Egyptian government officials and workers, and "qualified" researchers.

The completion of this tomb replication project will be a major step in further erasing the memory of a Black Egypt. These replica tombs, with the lightened colours and remade facial features, will graphically demonstrate that the evidence of classical African civilisations is vanishing. This of course, holds true for the Minoan and all other black civilisations.

This is by no means a deep history lesson. This is a short! Sharp! Shot of self-esteem to give you confidence in the fact that you are decedents of leaders and rulers of great kingdoms and empires.

You are worthy of riches and more than capable of leading your own nation. So let the knowledge of your great story help you strive to achieve your true status and riches in the world once again.

We have spoken about the African Holocaust and its legacy, slave mentality, all of the nasty details of the terrorist systems that control us, and their impact.

Now its time to bring to the forefront of your mind the greatness and grandeur of your African story, because that is what we are, great Africans.

Take your mind back to an aspect of your story where black people were rich, and had great kingdoms and empires.

We, as in black people, were organised, worked collectively and ruled ourselves as a nation. We created and manufactured products and then traded to supply the rest of the world.

When Maya Angelo's said; "For Africa to me ... is more than a glamorous fact. It is a historical truth. No man can know where he is going unless he knows exactly where he has been and exactly how he arrived at his present place."

It can be interpreted to mean, we cannot progress if we do not know our true history.

It is important to know your true history of greatness, power and wealth, and in so doing, you will feel confident in who you are.

Proud to be black and be inspired to achieve great things today, in the knowledge that you are descendants of the original human being, and the creators of great civilisations.

We have already established through the work and research of ProfessorManu Ampim that Ancient Egyptians were black people, that constructed and produced mind-blowing, complex architecture such as the pyramids and temples.

And they, as your ancestors are responsible for providing the world with reading and writing, mathematics, religion, philosophy, art and science. Some historians now admit to believing that Egypt influenced Greek scholars, and as such, the common works of Plato and Aristotle were based upon Egyptian scholarship.

It is so very important to claim what is rightfully ours and ancient Egypt is one such claim that we must own and promote as belonging to us.

African's International Trading Networks

Being organised, working collectively with each other, and trading with others is not a new concept, we did it in the past. We had thousands of years of rich history and culture before the African Holocaust.

The Mali Empire was one of the most significant cultural and trading focal points of West Africa, boasting impressive cities, including Timbuktu, with grand palaces, mosques and universities. Eleventh century Timbuktu, people travelled to learn in our universities.

The Mali empire supplied the worlds gold. Egypt and Nubia traded resources and gold. The trading of gold, copper, wood, cloth and other things across African civilisations, were common place.

Africans controlled extensive international trading networks and in trans-oceanic travel. Ninth century East Africa (Indian ocean) traded between Africa and Asia.

The Moors, who were the dominant people in Africa around 700-1300 CE established many civilisations and kingdoms at that time, building southern Europe in its entirety. They also brought order to the Iberian as well as the North Africa region.

Sixth century Ghana, your ancestors' created and manufactured products and then traded to supply the rest of the world, and controlled trade between Sudan and the Shara.

King Mansa Musa - the Richest Man in the Word; King Mansa Musa I (Emperor Moses) was a Malian king, ruling from 1312 to 1337 and expanding the Mali influence over the Niger city-states of Timbuktu, Gao, and Djenne.

Musa ruled the Mali Empire and was estimated to have been worth the equivalent of $400 billion in today's currency, which makes him the richest man to ever walk this earth.

The emperor was a master businessman and economist, and gained his wealth through Mali's supply of gold, salt and ivory, the main commodities for most of the world during that time. Musa maintained a huge army that kept peace and policed the trade routes for his businesses.

His armies pushed the borders of Mali from the Atlantic coast in the West; beyond the cities of Timbuktu and Gao in the East; and from the salt mines of Taghaza in the North to the gold mines of Wangar in the South.

Musa was also a major influence on the University of Timbuktu, the world's first university and the major learning institution for not just of Africa but the world.

Timbuktu became a meeting place of poets, scholars and artists of Africa and the Middle East. Even after Mali declined, Timbuktu remained the major learning centre of Africa for many years. When we were invaded we hid our books deep in the sand to protect our knowledge.

The richest man to ever walk the earth, clearly Musa was a genius economist and business man in addition to his other outstanding qualities, be proud of him.

The European Greed for Gold

It was gold from the great empires of West Africa, such as Ghana, Mali and Songhay, which provided the means for the economic take off of Europe in the 13th and 14th centuries and aroused the interest of Europeans in western Africa. Indeed it was the wealth of West Africa, especially as a source of gold, that encouraged the voyages of the early European explorers.

The international trade networks of West Africa peaked the interest of Europeans, and they found the overall wealth of gold from the great empires of West Africa even more so intriguing.

It was gold from the great empires of West Africa that prompted the early Portuguese voyages of exploration and ultimately enabled the economic catapult of Europe. Upon which our ancestors made the misguided decision to welcome the Portuguese with open arms as buyers in the fourteenth-fifteenth century.

They came to Africa to gain control of the entire African trade. They wrecked, looted and burned cities to the ground and turned your people into commodities. The very people that today have the audacity to call you gangsters and hoodlums, but who themselves are really the original hoodlums.

The African Holocaust was a major interruption to our nation that we should not forget. However we also have to remember what we were like, and how we behaved before it.

Despite popular belief, our rich history started prior to being enslaved, we were kings and queens of great civilisations.

However the conditioning, propaganda and brain-washing that has taken place over centuries will have you believe that you are a lesser human being and have not made any contribution to society.

On the contrary, The original men of civilisation were Black people, Africans. Africans come from civilisations highly developed on the African continent that produced science, scientists and great industries.

You were once rich. Think rich and be rich!

The Blacknificient 8, read on…

CHAPTER FIVE

THE BLACKNIFICIENT 8

"We could write a whole book on the real history of our glorious superheroes, but here are just a few tasters, as it is essential to know just how great we were as a race. And we must use that knowledge as inspiration and guidance to be great once more." – Khadijah Ward

SuperHeroes

Superheroes are usually make-believe powerful, charismatic formidable leaders whom possess awesome skills, that inspire and rescue us from the baddies. They make us feel that anything is possible, we trust and believe in them, and we also strive to be like them.

So, whether you are young or old, male or female, I'm sure you need a superhero in your life, I know I do.

I must confess, my father was the very first real superhero in my life, from as far back as I can remember I looked up to that man as though he were a God. And we as black people need to start seeing our men and women as superheroes.

However, my father, along with any other black man I presume had competition with the mainstream white fictional superheroes. The emotional attachment that they instil in us with all the high level marketing, comic books, tell-lie-vision and today's blockbuster films, you find yourself selecting favourites from the choices that you are given, and the daddies of the world tend to get drowned out.

Unfortunately, as black people we haven't created any world-wide fictional superheroes, because we don't seem to be at that stage in our post-slavery journey where we are able to prioritise and cater to the specific nurturing requirements of our children's fantasies and imagination.

We don't have any current real life certified superheroes, leaders either, that all of our children and adults alike can look to for stimulation of our imagination and guidance towards unity, liberation and greatness.

However, we do have real-life superheroes of the past that have all been taken out by the system, and we should raise their profile, market, promote them to our children, follow their work and provide them the platform of the superhero status that they deserve.

Presenting in no particular order some of the Superheroes of our time that I like to call The Blacknificient 8…

1. **The legendary one and only Marcus Garvey (August 1887 - June 1940)**

" *We are going to emancipate ourselves from mental slavery because whilst others might free the body, none but ourselves can free the mind*" – Marcus Garvey

Garvey was unique in advancing a Pan-African philosophy to inspire a global mass movement and economic empowerment focusing on Africa.

Born in Jamaica, travelling to London and the US, Garvey aimed to organise black people everywhere but achieved his greatest impact in the United States, where he tapped into and enhanced the growing black aspirations for justice, wealth, and a sense of community.

Upon Garvey's arrival in New York City in1916 he noted that the black communities in northern cities could provide the wealth and unity to end both imperialism in Africa and discrimination in the United States and he created the Negro World Newspaper.

The Negro World was circulated weekly, established in 1918. The Negro Word was as a crucial tool in the fight for black liberation, as a specialised media outlet and tool to engage and empower black people — and to counter-act the negative propaganda of mainstream white media.

The paper had a distribution of upwards of five hundred thousand copies weekly at its peak, which included both subscribers and newspaper purchasers.

Negro World also played an important part in the Harlem Renaissance of the 1920s. The paper was a focal point for publication on the arts and African-American culture, including poetry, commentary on theatre and music, and regular book reviews.

During World War I and the 1920s, his Universal Negro Improvement Association (UNIA) was the largest black secular organisation in African-American history. Possibly a million men and women from the United States, the Caribbean, and Africa were members of Garvey's organisation.

Marcus Garvey combined the economic nationalist ideas of Booker T. Washington and Pan-Africanists with the political possibilities and urban style of men and women living outside of plantation and colonial societies.

Garvey's ideas gestated amid the social upheavals, anti-colonial movements, and revolutions of World War I, which demonstrated the power of popular mobilisation to change entrenched structures of power.

Garvey's goals were ambitious and ahead of his time. He sought to end imperialist rule and create modern societies in Africa.

With his newspaper the Negro World he united black communities on three continents and in 1919 formed the Black Star Line, an international shipping company to provide transportation and encourage trade among the black businesses of Africa and the Americas. In the same year, he founded the Negro Factories Corporation to establish such businesses. In 1920 he presided over the first of several international conventions of the UNIA. Garvey sought to channel the new black militancy into one organisation that could overcome class and national divisions.

Although local UNIA chapters provided many social and economic benefits for their members, Garvey's main efforts failed: the Black

Star Line suspended operations in 1922 and the other enterprises fared no better. Garvey's ambition and determination to lead inevitably collided with associates and black leaders in other organisations.

His verbal talent and flair for the dramatic attracted thousands,

Our Black Superheroes are deemed enemies of the state, as black liberation is a threat to its existence. Thus, drastic measures will be taken to try and stop our superheroes from realising the dream.

For Marcus Garvey it was J. Edgar Hoover, the then director of the FBI who was his nemesis. Hoover closely followed the movements of Garvey and three other UNIA officials whom were eventually charged with mail fraud involving the Black Star Line. That is all that Hoover could get on him.

On June 23, 1923, Garvey was convicted and sentenced to prison for five years. Claiming to be a victim of a politically motivated miscarriage of justice, Garvey appealed his conviction, but was denied. In 1927 he was released from prison and deported to Jamaica.

Garvey continued his political activism and the work of UNIA in Jamaica, and then moved to London in 1935.

Through all of Garvey's battles he brought together a race that had no direction and gave them hope and opportunity. Even though, he was forced to leave the United States he accomplished the largest black movement in history.

This visionary and economic genius, was a remarkable man of his time, and no man to-date has matched the accomplishments of this remarkable visionary. He truly is a superhero, second to none, and n inspiration for us all. You must all draw inspiration and mirror the work of your incredible pioneer.

2. Fred Hampton - Black Panther August 30, 1948 – December 4, 1969 (Assassinated)

"*We're going to fight racism not with racism, but we're going to fight with solidarity. We say we're not going to fight capitalism with black capitalism, but we're going to fight it with socialism.*" – Fred Hampton

Fred Hampton was born in Chicago. Fred Hampton, Wow! To me he is a special kind of Superhero, due to his numerous accomplishments up until his assassination at the tender age of twenty-one.

A bright student, Hampton graduated from Proviso East High School in 1966 before enrolling at Triton Junior College where he studied law.

Hampton became active in the civil rights movement whilst still a student. He joined the National Association for the Advancement of Coloured People (NAACP) and was appointed leader of the Youth Council of the organisation's West Suburban branch.

In 1965 Hampton emerged at the charismatic chairman of The Black Panther Party. Originally formed to protect local communities from police brutality and racism, it eventually developed into a revolutionary group.

The group also ran medical clinics and provided free food to school children. Hampton founded the Chicago chapter of the Black Panther Party in November 1968. He immediately established a community service program.

This included the provision of free breakfasts for schoolchildren and a medical clinic that did not charge patients for treatment. He instigated a community control of police project and also taught political education classes. In fact, one of his rules were that if you wanted to become a member of the panthers you would have to undertake the political education classes first.

The activities of the Black Panthers in Chicago came to the attention of, wait for it… J. Edgar Hoover and the FBI.

Hoover described the Panthers as "the greatest threat to the internal security of the country." Can you believe that, 'the greatest threat to the internal security of the country'. A man that is fighting against injustice from the system, and working to unite and uplift his people is seen by the highest levels of government as a national security threat.

The FBI mind-set is a clear demonstration that the global white power structure has the 'black fear' syndrome and are completely afraid that the black man will one day take back his power and wealth.

J.Edgar Hoover wanted the work of the panthers disrupted, destroyed and neutralised by any means necessary to prevent the rise of what they described as a Messiah that could unify and electrify the black masses. Again, you see, they do not want the black masses unified it scares them, they know what can be accomplished through unity. As we have discussed throughout this book unity is the key to power and economic collective wealth.

Hoover urged Chicago police to launch an all-out assault on the panther organisation, which led to the conspiracy of Hampton's assassination by the FBI, the Chicago police and the attorney's office.

In the early hours of the December 4, 1969, the ruthless pigs raided the Panther headquarters for the fourth time and Fred Hampton was shot execution style at point blank range through the head right where he lay in his bed with a his finance next to him who at the time was eight months pregnant. He was just 21 years old.

In my mind the most significant achievement that gives Hampton the superhero status, is his age, and that at that young age he persuaded Chicago's most powerful street gangs to stop fighting against each other. That is not an easy task which takes special skills.

In May 1969 Hampton held a press conference where he announced a nonaggression pact between the gangs and the formation of what he called a "rainbow coalition" a multiracial alliance of black, Puerto Rican, and poor youths.

For his young years he was able to effectively engage with a wide spectrum of people from mothers on welfare, to college students, business people, gang kids and pull all people together . He made people believe in themselves and he made people feel powerful. Hampton could, and did bring about change that was his charisma and tremendous leadership.

3. Muhammed Ali, 'Float like a Butterfly Sting Like a Bee' (17/01/42 - 03/06/16)

A fearless revolutionary political figure and outspoken activist "I'm the greatest - I said that even before I knew I was" – Muhammed Ali

Ali oozed charisma and self-confidence. Fearless, highly intelligent and a way with words that exceeds the description of articulation. He was indeed is a great example of someone who consciously fought to rid themselves of a slave mentality and openly opposed the system.

Growing up in the segregated south of USA, he experienced racial prejudice and discrimination firsthand. He used his high-profile, celebrity status to bring the issues of racism to the forefront at the height of the civil rights movement.

It would have been very easy for Muhammed Ali to collect his millions and not say a word about the plight of the black man, like some famous black celebrities of today in entertainment and sport who say and do nothing regarding progressing the black cause of independence.

However, Mohammed Ali wasn't afraid. He understood the repercussions of his words, yet his principles compelled him to speak and take precedence over his career within a white system.

He stood fast in the face of the systems fury, he stood up to the USA government and did not compromise his principles for fame and money.

When Ali refused to join the Army because of his religious beliefs and opposition to the Vietnam War it created quite a nationwide controversy. He said:

"If I'm going to die I'm going to die right here fighting you, my enemy are white people not Viet cons or Chinese or Japanese. You're my opposer, when I want freedom, you my opposer when I want justice, you my opposer when I want equality. You wont even stand up for me and my religious beliefs, you want me to go and fight but you wont even stand up."

"My conscience wont let me go and shoot some darker people, or poorer people for what....They never called me nigger they never lynched me, they never put no dogs on me."

He was stripped of his world title and banned from boxing for three and a half years — the power of the system at work but it did not faze him. Ali's articulation and fearlessness was his power, however Ali was ultimately silenced. The supposed parkinson's disease took away his speech —Ali once said what boxer you know gets parkinson's and loses his speech.

Muhammed Ali has been mentioned a few times in this book, because he is to be admired and used as an inspiration of self-love and fearlessness.

4. MALCOLM X 19 May 1925 - 21 February1965 (Assassinated)

"*The Black man has to be reeducated to the importance of supporting Black business, but the Black man himself has to be made aware of the importance of going into business. Once you and I go into business we own and operate at least the businesses in our own community. We will be developing a situation wherein we will be able to create employment for the people in the community. Once we create employment it will eliminate the necessity of having to act ignorantly and disgracefully boycotting some c*****r some place else trying to beg him for a job...Anytime you have to rely upon your enemy for a job you are in bad shape.*" – Malcolm X

The erudite, verbally dexterous, orator and charismatic genius…Malcolm X. Boy I wish I was grown when he was alive. He was a revolutionary, of uncompromising political consciousness, who pressed for black community control and independence with black-owned businesses 'doing for self.'

He mastered the English dictionary, by heart, commanding authority and respect with his articulate deployment of words and charismatic leadership style.

Malcolm was skilled in public debate and held his own against political and intellectual adversaries on campuses and in broadcast studios. He consistently expressed views ridiculing civil rights leaders and their integrationist assumptions.

His loyalty to his people could not be wavered which was demonstrated when the FBI tried to recruit him to work for them and he vehemently declined.

He has been described as one of the greatest and most influential African Americans in history. Credited with raising the self-esteem of black Americans and reconnecting them with their African heritage.

He is largely responsible for the spread of Islam in the black community in the United States.

Through the Nation of Islam, Malcolm X created economic control, building up Black communities with industry, stores and mosques driving out drug dealers and criminals. Today the Nation of Islam owns hundreds of businesses nationwide and operates its own farm to support its members.

Malcolm X should undoubtedly give you inspiration to aspire to self-reliance, in Black unity, and economic wealth and power.

5. Queen Nzingha (1583-1663) 'Bad Ass' Warrior

Queen Nzingha or "Amazon Queen of Matamba" was born in West Africa. She was the one and only fearless warrior Queen and military genius. Many women ranked among the great rulers of Africa, including this Angolian Queen who was an astute diplomat and excelled as a military leader.

When the slave-hunting Portuguese attacked the army of her brother's kingdom, She formed her own army against the Portuguese, fighting on the front-line waging war for nearly thirty years, uniting Africans against the Portuguese. She fought off colonisation; built an empire making her land a centre of trade which made her country powerful (equal to Portuguese colonies).

Creating wealth and business she kept her land independent and free up until the nineteenth century. Queen Nzingha had it all; Leadership, Royalty, Military genius. And last but not least, fearless warrior and entrepreneur empire builder.

Now that's a 'bad ass' Superhero! Take some lessons people!

6. Sonni Ali Songhai Empire

Sonni Ali (The Great) Founder and King of the Songhai Empire 15th -16th Century.

With Sonni at the helm, The Songhai Empire became the largest Muslim West African Empire of all time. Trained in political and Military science Sonni, also known as Sonni Ali the Great was a brilliant military mind and led the largest imperialist mission in West Africa.

His first major conquest occurred the in following year when the Muslim leaders of Timbuktu, one of the great cities of the Mali Empire, asked for help against the Tuareg, the nomadic desert Berbers who had occupied the city since 1433. Sonni Ali took the opportunity not only to strike decisively against the Tuareg but also against the city itself.

Timbuktu became part of the Songhai Empire in 1469. Sonia's forces were amphibious, attacking and patrolling by land and water, down the Niger River.

During his reign, the Songhai Empire reached its pinnacle, surpassing the Great Mali Empire, absorbing its territories and the famed city Timbuktu. There are no more words necessary here, the greatness of this man speaks for itself.

7. Queen Nanny - Jamaican Heroine

(1686 Ghana - 1733 Jamaica)

The legendary Queen Nanny of the Jamaican Maroons is one of the most celebrated, but least recognised figures outside of Jamaica in the resistance history of the New World. She mastered the art of unifying people.

She was a queen captured in her homeland, forcefully transported across the Atlantic Ocean in the belly of a slave ship. In the New

World she would eventually rise up to become the leader of a new nation and create unity among the people.

'Nanny,' warrior chieftains of the Jamaican Maroons, led a band of former enslaved Africans in the rugged mountains of Jamaica to a decisive victory over the mighty British army during the early to mid-18th century. — military genius-

A strong fearless leader that she was, she used african culture to unite the people, people that were from different parts of Africa speaking different languages. She organised into several community groups trained their people in guerrilla warfare, and kept people free and independent. The maroons have never been enslaved.

Take lessons people! From our unsung hero Queen Nanny, highly skilful in organisation, unity and leadership of people.

8. **Taharqa - Nubian King**

Taharqa is probably one of the most famous rulers of Napatan Kush, reigning from 690 to 664 B.C.

This great Nubian king is more than worthy of his superhero status having led his armies against the invading Assyrians at just sixteen years of age.

During his 25-year rule, Taharqa controlled the largest empire in ancient Africa. His power was equaled only by the Assyrians.

These two forces were in constant conflict, but despite continuous warfare, Taharqa was able to initiate a building program throughout his empire, which was overwhelming in scope.

The number and majesty of his building projects were legendary, with the greatest being the temple at Gebel Barkal in the Sudan. The temple was carved from rock and decorated with images of Taharqa over 100 feet high.

Compare what our sixteen year-olds today are doing to what sixteen year-old Taharqa was doing back then. We need to promote him to our young people as a superhero they need to emulate.

Remember, you are descendent of a Noble race. Your ancestors were royal, leaders, empire builders, leaders, great inventors, scientists, creators, educators and warriors. Black people, you are the original people of the world, know the history of your race, know it and be proud of it.

Are you seeing a pattern here? The qualities, characteristics and achievements of your ancestors are second to none. Royal, military genius, entrepreneurial genius, empire building, wealth, pride, dignity and the list goes on.

Imagine what it must have been like in those times to live and experience being part of such a noble and great race.

You were Noble and you were Kings and Queens! Get to know the rich and real history of your race. Understanding the achievements and inventions of your ancestors, that will give you a sense of personal power.

Young Black people of today do not understand that our existence started long before the slave trade, you must educate them, let them know that we were rulers, inventors, surgeons, money makers and masters of business. We were Kings and Queens of a great nation that other races have tried to replicate today and failed miserably.

Self-reliance goes without saying. Your ancestors would not depend upon the hand-outs of a white power structure and you should not either. Be conscious of your true history and be proud to be all that is black. Let the knowledge of our super heroes inspire you in the face of adversity and let us be reunited in greatness.

Black Sterling Action Step 5 Resurrect our Superheroes.

This action may seem somewhat weird but we need to be able to raise the profile of our superheroes.

Our history is rich with royalty and filled with visionary's and leaders that have overcome in the face of adversity. They are pioneers of economic and military power and social organisation in action, you must seriously be inspired by them to be great once more.

Talk to your children about them and remember them and their great work so we can look to them for guidance and help from beyond the grave in our current journey of unity , black liberation, self-reliance and economic wealth.

Without unity we will perish, read on…

CHAPTER SIX

WITHOUT UNITY YOU WILL PERISH

"Ignorance of each other is what has made unity impossible in the past. Therefore we need enlightenment. We need more light about each other. Light creates understanding, understanding creates love, love creates patience, and patience creates unity. Once we have more knowledge (light) about each other, we will stop condemning each other and a United front will be brought about." – Malcolm X

Strategically Respond - Or Emotionally React?

I'm going to give you two examples of when black people have united in an emotional reaction to issues.

1. The 1985 Brixton Riots caused by the Police raid and shooting of Cherry Groce.

2. The 2011 Tottenham Riots, in retaliation to the Murder by shooting of Mark Duggan by Police forces.

I was present on both occasions, and it's understandable in both situations why black people would react in the way that they did. It was 'just deserts' and it felt good to vent anger and frustration.

However emotional reactions have short term outcomes, leaving you caught up in the very same system that you find yourselves retaliating against.

The point of the two examples were to demonstrate that we can come together in unity if we really want to, but we only tend to do so in an emotional reaction when we have reached the end of our tether. When in actual fact our unity should be strategic and thought out with military precision.

So, regarding our current situation, you know the one where we are getting screwed each and every day by the system. Wouldn't it make sense to be proactive as opposed to reactive and unite in a strategic manner to deliver real everyday positive outcomes in the lives of our people, and to prevent or if not minimise negative treatments towards us.

I'm going to go out on a limb here and answer my own question. Yes, it would! Unity, social organisation and strategic planning to deliver long term effective and measurable outcomes are essential but the first step must be unity.

Why the hell is she talking about Ants!

You may well ask yourself. Well, I am in awe of the ant and here is the reason why...Let me tell you a quick story.

On a hot summer's day in the white suburbs of kelvin road, in Highbury London, United Kingdom 1968, a young black child playing hopscotch on the pavement looked down and saw an ant crawling out of a tiny hole in the ground.

Upon its head it carried a small piece of stone, concrete, part of the pavement, the image seemed equivalent to a man carrying a massive concrete boulder upon his shoulders.

As she continued to watch in awe of this tiny creature, an army of ants followed the first ant in a succinct line of organised fashion with military precision. They all did the same, carrying the concrete on top of their heads across the pavement travelling to a destination to build whatever it was, only they knew the answer.

The child looking on at ants in action was me, and from that day forth that image of an army of ants working collectively has remained etched in my memory.

I wondered, how could they be so tiny and insignificant but yet operate like the military, and co-exist in the grand scheme of the world with such highly developed social organisation and systems. To this day I have been fascinated by the brain power of such tiny creatures.

High Level Social Organisers

The success of ants throughout the world has been attributed to their high level social organisation with their talents to modify habitats, tap resources, and defend themselves.

The ant parallels with human society in that they are organised and methodical with divisions of labour, communication accompanied by an ability to solve complex problems.

Ants tend to operate as a unified entity, collectively working together to support the colonies that range in size from a few dozen to highly organised colonies that may occupy large territories and consist of millions of individuals.

Just for a moment really study the ant, how they live and operate alongside humans but function within their own systems and processes to their benefit.

Ants have mastered the art of collective organisation and unity thus creating a powerful co-existence on the planet.

I ask you this, if tiny ants can unite and organise themselves with military precision to achieve common goals, why can't the black man do it also?

We, the human species that are supposed to be critical thinkers, superior to animals and creatures, and we, the first human beings to have graced the plant.

Come on Now, it is Time to Up Your Game!

Imagine, if we, just like the ant began to think and act collectively. Those of you whom are reading this book, spread the word amongst your friends and family and united in the first instance with the whole black community from across the UK and developed a strategic plan to build wealth for your people.

For example, just as a start, you started to pool together centrally just £10 from each and every one of you, how much money could you accumulate to start building businesses and industries for and in your community?

Answer: £19,046,840. That figure derives from the amount of 'Black British' people recorded from the 2011 Census. That number multiplied by ten is a vast amount of money to begin to create an economic revolution.

In the 2001 Census, 565,876 people in the UK had reported their ethnicity as "Black Caribbean," 485,277 as "Black African," and 97,585 as "Black Other," making a total of 1,148,738 "Black or Black British" residents. This was supposedly equivalent to two per cent of the UK population at the time.

The 2011 census showed Black British as 1,904,684. We may be recorded as three percent of the population, but we are still large in number when you look at the black community as a whole, which is more than enough of you in the population to contribute to a plan of action for a black economic system.

Imagine, I say imagine a lot because the imagination is a powerful tool, the subconscious that enables us to produce dreams and fantasy to ultimately create reality, and I for one love to use it.

Imagine, if united in your aims like the ant, and, as a start, you pooled your money together and also started spending as a priority with black-owned businesses, buying and selling products and services from each other what could be achieved.

Money would circulate within your own community, increasing your wealth. Wealth that could be directed to building big industries within your own community.

Small shops could become big department stores, we could build free schools where children are taught to succeed, with pride in who they are.

We could create finance institutions, private hospitals, build housing corporations through our own construction companies and corporations that create job opportunities for our own people.

We could also direct our own funds and wealth to eradicate gun crime and drug use of our young people.

We could create rehabilitation programmes that work for our young men, and women for that matter, when they are released from jail to ensure that they never return.

We can end unemployment and self destructive behaviour by creating wealthy communities that our young people feel proud and want to be a part of.

A community where they feel that drugs and crime is not the only salvation. The list is endless, but it can only happen if you think We, not me, and We Unite as a race of people.

Wealth and Unity equals Power

Only when you, and each and every one of us unite as a race to liberate from the mental chains of slavery, will our revolution be achieved.

The statistics would suggest that our combined numbers and spending power can build wealth. You are an economic revolution waiting to happen.

Collective wealth is the source of power in communities, and the system stops the black community from gaining that power and wealth by killing, incarceration and overall control of your movements throughout the system.

If we are doing drugs, locked up or dead you cannot aspire to wealth and power, or even function productively as a community. Or if you are fortunate enough not to be caught up in any of those things we are programmed not to support and unite with our own.

White people think collectively, and act as a unit, that is crystal clear from the racist systems that we live under. The entire infrastructure and its systems would not be effective without the collective thought and action of unity of the white masses.

Through unity and the production of black economic self-reliance you would also have the power to control the politics in your community. As they say, 'money talks' and that is the name of the game in politics.

Wealth has to be a collective in order to hold any power and control in politics. And wealth scratches each others back.

The Competitive Advantage of the White Man

The main reason that white people are able to dominate society and have an abundance of wealth is that use of their competitive advantage which is unity. They all buy-in to the same ideals and work together through their systems to realise them.

If they stop practicing unity then their competitive advantage over the black community will cease. It took the unity of them all to introduce the institution of slavey, and all of their other established institutions and infrastructures which is paramount to enable systems to work successfully and could not work without the buy-in and co-operation from the people.

The institution of banking has been established since slavery and due to slavery. Barclays bank for example was founded during the slave period, in 1690.

Banking is the over-arching institution set up to control your money, it is an all white institution and the controllers of the system work together to keep it that way, because banking equals power and wealth, that is the systems design.

Even though there are established different banks, banking is a collective institution, governed by all the same laws and regulations, which allows it to let certain people in and exclude others. You will find that black people do not own banks, well at least not here in the UK. You have been shut out of banking as an owner, your role is solely as a consumer to enable the bank to function on the basis of your money.

It is tied to government and politics, a selective system to ensure that wealth, politics and power go hand-in-hand. Remember the banking crisis in 2007 the government bailed out the banks and you and I are still footing the bill.

The controllers of the system work in unity to secure the power, govern, make law and circulate the wealth between the institutions that they own.

The vast majority of UK politicians and bankers to-date have come from privileged backgrounds. They have money. They have attended the same schools and colleges and 'daddy' has paved the way for their political careers.

I am sure you are familiar the character James Bond 007, right. Well the guy behind James Bond's creation was a British guy Ian Fleming, he wrote the spy novel series in the 1950s.

Fleming attended Eton university, he was an English author, journalist and he worked for Britain's Naval Intelligence Division. He came from a wealthy family connected to the merchant bank Robert Fleming & Co. And his father was the Member of Parliament.

Let's just analyse Fleming for a moment. He went to an elite university in Britain, namely Eton, he came from wealth, his family were in

Banking, one of if not the most powerful institutions in Britain. His father was also an MP, lots of influence there to connect with decision-makers and secure favours. He was able to make time to write novels and secure publishing contracts for his books.

The life of this individual was mapped out for success because the system is designed, for his kind to receive the best possible opportunities to succeed and live happy and prosperous lives.

Ex UK Prime Minister David Cameron and ex Mayor of London, Boris Johnson, both attended Oxford another elite university, and shared the same classroom.

Have you noticed any real intelligence in either of them? I certainly haven't, they are intellectual light-weights as far as I am concerned, yet both have reached powerful standards of political careers. That's skin-colour, money, wealth, unity and connections that put them there, not intelligence.

Politics, big corporations and industries operate through collective wealth and unity of the people operating the system. They help each other get rich and stay rich and they understand the basics of that system which cannot work without the unity of those of whom it benefits.

You see the patterns within the system must be understood in order to recreate systems of your own. And to reiterate it must be a collective effort. You black people must work in unity.

Previously we discussed some celebrity status and ordinary individuals having vast amounts of wealth that have failed to unite in common interests and centralise their wealth to build industry for black communities.

The wealth of an individual, when used solely for the purposes of that individual serves only that individual, which is meaningless from the perspective of the black community. That is evident from the many millionaires that we have, but yet we do not have a collective black economic system.

We have further established the vast 'spending power' of the Black community in Britain which is an immense economic wealth, that is currently failing to circulate within your community.

Unity of people with a strategic plan would enable collective wealth to create our own banks, housing corporations, factories, corporations, education and financial institutions and any other significant industries.

Whereas failure to adopt a collective frame of mind and establish unity will see the black nation ultimately perish, as the current situation of the black community is clearly unsustainable.

You are nearing the end of this book, Black Sterling, and this entire book has provided you with information about the racist system that beguiles and slays you and your children, with further evidence that integration into the system has purposely failed you as a nation.

It has also shown you that you cannot ask the people that inflict racism upon you to stop that racism, and give you equality, pride, dignity and opportunity. It is a foolish notion indeed that we must realise shall never come to pass.

Throughout this book you have also seen evidence that black people as a race are powerless under this current regime of the euro-centric infrastructures.

Therefore, black people must unite as a nation to operate within an alternative system, a black economic system. We must build infrastructures of your own from which you all benefit and acquire economic control, power and wealth. That is the only course of action left to the people both you and I.

Black Sterling Action Step 5

UNIFY : This is just another step towards your independent black economic system and collective wealth. I recommend uniting your skills, knowledge and experience by:

a) Working with the BlackSterling Nation Building Team (contact khadijah ward on Facebook to request joining the team).

b) Start your own community group.

c) Join a local group in your community.

CHAPTER SEVEN

TAKE IT **BLACK**

"I voted for Obama because he was black, 'Cuz that's why other folks vote for other people — because they look like them." – Samuel L. Jackson

"You should take heed and adopt that same principle as Samuel L. Jackson, we must shop with black-owned businesses because they are black. Period! I do it, other races do it and so should you." – Khadijah Ward

Do Owners of Pak have Afros?

"These products, which are vital for maintaining healthier hair and skin, are generally not available at most high street shops in the UK or Europe, However, thanks the support of millions of consumers like you. We have successfully grown our business, from that small acorn, to Europe's leading Afro retailer ,with seven renowned specialty centre in the UK." A statement made by Pak the UK Multi-Million pound Asian-owned black hair care and beauty corporation

This chapter is about taking back industries that by rights belong to us. The first industry and main focus of this chapter is the black hair care and beauty industry.

Why is it that black people are the only race that not only watch all the other races get rich while we stand by, but also allow other races to get rich from us while we stay poor?

The multimillion pound Asian-owned black haircare and beauty chain describe themselves as follows on their website. "*Specialising in African and African Caribbean hair and beauty products for today's Fashion conscious consumer, established just over 27 years ago, our family run destination icon for millions of African's and African Caribbean's all over Africa, Europe and the Caribbean who regularly rely on PAK Cosmetic Centre's for products, specifically developed for Afro consumers.*"

How many of the Pak owners have afros? None! They are not black. It's ludicrous, isn't it? Pak, is thanking you, black people for making them wealthy. That statement should give you the incentive to support black-owned businesses as a priority, and purchase your hair products exclusively from black-owned businesses.

As the Pak statement says, millions of you have supported their growth, which means there are more than enough of you to support the growth of black-owned hair care businesses. Am I right?

Do you think that Asian people would purchase Asian specific products from black people? Would Asian people buy their Saris or Shalwar Kameez from you? Would they buy their indian take-away curry from you?

Absolutely not! Why? Because they are Asian specific products. And as Asian people their mentality is collective, they believe that Asian people should create wealth for their own community and profit from their own products and services, and quite rightly so.

So Who is Selling to the Black Consumer?

Fact 1! The black nation allows other races to take our black products, sell them back to us and make millions and billions in the process as we stay poor, right! And that makes you, the black community consumers for the system and major contributors to the UK economy but you are not the benefactors.

Fact 2! We allow our industries to be taken away from us because the system has programmed us to be a divided people, brain-washed to the point that we do not we see our own black-owned businesses as a negative and we do not support them.

Fact 3! We are programmed to be high level consumers for others and not business owners. So, when some of us take the plunge and become business owners, our fellow man will not support us due to the sophisticated programming under the system that makes us reject any such notion. We are commodities of the system and that does not include being successful business owners.

Some may say, well that's not true there are lots of successful black-owned businesses out there. That, my dear brothers and sisters is the sophistication of the system, it gives you some crumbs, tiny benefits from it to make you believe that the system is working in your favour.

The system can take a small portion of you being successful, but not an entire nation. Those black-owned businesses that you see are operating in isolation not as a collective unit of the community. And you, are programmed to ensure that it stays that way by not supporting them with your money.

Tell me that I am wrong. You cannot. Just take a look around you and see who is controlling black products and making huge profits. Who are the consumers supporting the non-black owned business that market and sell black products?

Who are the people that apply massive criticism on black-owned businesses and use every excuse in the book not to support them? Who are the people that prevent micro black-owned businesses from becoming large industries?

The answer to those questions is that is you, black people. And this chapter is all about taking back the industries that belong to us starting now!

We are aware that brands such as Tropical Sun that markets and sells Caribbean spices and other products is an Asian-owned brand but their consumer target market is the black community.

The restaurant chain called Turtle Bay that specialises in selling Caribbean dishes is not owned by black people, but black people are the frequented customers.

Pak, an Asian-owned Black hair care store started from a tiny shop in Stroud Green Road London, and has grown into a massive superstore from the money of the Black woman.

I have mentioned three, but that is the tip of the ice-burg. The issues of other races targeting the black community as consumers and getting rich off the back of you is the same across the world.

Major brands, write books, undertake extensive research on black consumer spending and share information with their white business peers to help them successfully target the black consumer, which in all fairness should be your consumer.

The Secret of Selling to the Negro

I can take you back as far as the nineteen fifties when America publicly declared their consumer targeting campaign toward the black community.

The 'Secret of selling to the Negro' was a 1954 American TV production in cooperation with the US department of commerce.

The documentary focused upon what they called a new market that was bound to have a terrific impact for business. Billion and billions of new prospects with $15 billion to spend. A fresh market full of opportunities, blew up so fast that they didn't even realise its scope, they said.

A neglected market with money waiting to be spent. To be able to tell you the secret of selling to the negro, they said they did a lot of digging. They talked to the local business men. They went to Washington DC and set up cameras and other key points around the nation to observe the 'negro' their new consumer.

Out of their observations emerged a story of a new market. Yes, this is the market we are talking about the new negro family, they said, as they showed images of black families.

Their names are Wells or Wilson, Smith or Brown, they live in Atlanta, Chicago or New York, Detroit St Louis, Los Angeles etcetera. They have new interests, new standards of living a buying power they have never had before. They are good prospects for all types of goods and services. So why let old fashioned ideas hurt profits, they said.

The US secretary of commerce of that time appeared on the documentary. Alerting people to trends that mean a national healthy economy, better business for the nation as a whole.

"We are interested in a rising young market that shows huge potential for goods and services I am referring to the new negro market."

"The tremendous buying power of this group is at a record high, since 1939 it has increased by more than all other americans. Here is a buying power that cannot help but have a positive effect on our national economy and business prosperity in general." This is what the then US secretary of commerce said whilst they showed figures of income and wages.

When these dollars are spent on goods and services, businesses everywhere are bound to feel the impact.

A product cannot be number one without negro support, it must have the backing of this big new buying power. They'll buy from anyone who wants to sell to them.

You must first understand about them, what do they buy, how do they buy, and why do they buy.

It went on to say the secret of selling to the negro is one word, recognition. People want to be recognised they need recognition, because he has had so little of it the negro needs even more than others.

He needs to feel important and appreciated. This needs shows in the negro's shopping habits. Anyone who wants to sell to the negro customer should know about these habits.

They explained three habits in particular that they believe play a part in every sales transaction.

1. Most 'Negros' buy by brand, they ask for products by name. They are quick to turn down off brands.

2. Quality merchandise. Symbols of quality and prestige are very important to the negro customer they buy the approval of their friends and relatives.

It is a well known fact that many 'Negros' are influenced by the opinion of others. What their friends may think of a certain item will usually determine whether or not a sale is made.

3. When he asks for one thing don't try to sell him something else. If you do he'll probably react something like this. " doesn't he think I have the money to pay for it" There is a reason for this reaction, they

said, because he is used to cheap merchandise he resents being offered a substitute to the quality brand that he has now chosen.

The 'negro' family does things as a group, and lives as a unit and buys as a unit. Sell to one and sell to all it's a pre sold market.

Use black publications as advertising mediums to reach the negro customer, such as ebony magazine which has been effective in bringing sales. And don't talk to the negro about race, religion or politics just stick to the sale.

White People Got You Sussed!

From the documentary 'The secret of selling to the Negro' you can see that the white man has accessed your psyche and identified you as a community that likes to spend money and why and how you do it. And I quote, "They will buy from anyone who wants to sell to them."

There is nothing wrong in spending money, however there is a problem when that money is directed away from your own community in an abundance.

You can also see that they are trying to sell the black man to the white business owner as a consumer that they should target by creating a rapport of similarity. Hence the mention of the black people's names that are the same as theirs, Smith, Wilson, Brown etcetera. Remember in the 'slave mentality' chapter where we spoke about how white people prefer to identify with you when you have european names.

They were also talking about how the black man is overlooked as consumers due to out of date ideas about how they live and how he buys. They were showing that the black man lives the same as other 'folks' as they put it and he buys the same.

They were trying to remove the image that black people were previously known as drifters, poor credit risks and dregs of society which previously prevented people wanting to do business with them.

There were two points of this documentary that stood out for me. One, was that they understood that we purchased as a unit, a family therefore they sold to the entire family, and most importantly it shows that they understood the power of unity.

Secondly, the documentary stated that, and I quote "*A product cannot be number one without negro support, it must have the backing of this big new buying power.*" This demonstrates that they recognised the black community's economic spending power with every intention of capitalising on it.

These are the two points that you must take from this section of the book, if other people recognise this about you, then you must too.

1. You must operate as a unit.

2. You have the spending power to make products number one sellers, so you must direct this spending towards black-owned businesses to make your own people's products number one. Are you getting this people?

Let Me Tell You a Quick Story...

About The time I realised that non-black hair shops were exclusively selling black products to black people.

In the year of 1989 my sister and I wanted to buy hair grease and other hair care product items. We walked along Stroud Green Road, North London in the UK, and found a tiny shop called Pak, which turned out to be an Asian-owned Black hair care store.

Incidentally, today in 2017, Pak has grown into a massive superstore with a multi-million pound turnover from the money of the black consumer. And, in addition, they now own every black hair shop along Stroud Green Road.

Anyway, my sister and I walked in, and browsed around, and I was totally 'pissed off' that the person trying to advise me and sell me black products was not a black man, who, incidentally was telling me "this one is better for you," when I was assessing which hair grease to buy. I found that highly annoying! "Kiss me teet."

From then on, my sister and I made a conscious decision to boycott stores like Pak that are not black-owned, and, to spend our money exclusively with black-owned businesses.

Not because we have anything against Asian stores, but it is our belief that other races should not get rich off the back of black people, whilst we stay poor. Particularly with products, goods and services that are specific to us.

However, back in the day I was struggling with finding black-owned businesses that sold black products, although I eventually found an African-owned store in Peckham, South London, which I used exclusively and travelled from East London to buy from them, but at the same time I was getting more and more frustrated with other none-black owned businesses selling black products and services to me and my community.

I persevered and I actually sought out black-owned businesses not just for hair products but for other needs.

Black hair care and beauty is a billion pound industry that is not currently contributing towards the growth and well-being of the black community. On the contrary, it is making other communities rich and keeping your community poor.

And to add insult to injury, black people get treated like a piece of crap when you go and purchase from their shops, but I find black women are still purchasing from non-black owned stores without thinking about the economic consequences on the community. This has to stop.

We Got Cash but Don't Buy Black

Let me tell you a quick story about a close friend of mine Craig Cordice a gentleman and fine business man. I love a quick story, don't you?

Craig and I have worked closely together other the years on various projects, for instance the highly published 'Burning Injustice' campaign that we developed around the 2012 London Olympics.

The London Olympic Games was won on a commitment to diversity and equal opportunities and both Craig and I through our respective businesses tried to win contracts to deliver services to the Olympics.

However our efforts were in vain, as we soon came to realise that Black-owned and Asian businesses were being carved out of the Olympic contracts awards.

The Olympic Delivery Authority had £6bn worth of contracts for the London Organising Committee of the Olympic Games and Paralympic Games but only 6.3 percent of Black and Asian businesses were successful in winning contracts.

The people of colour in London were essentially used to win the Olympics but as the same old story goes the system controllers pocketed the billions of pounds for themselves and their friends with no intention of allowing us to reap the rewards. Well, only a token few.

I met Craig in 2006 when I started out as a business owner. I was at a business fare and he had commissioned a stall at the fare promoting his business and magazine called Engage.

I was immediately smitten by his vibrant personality, beautiful smile and the quality of his product. I immediately took out my cheque book and signed up for an annual subscription to his magazine.

The main reason I signed up to engage magazine is because Craig was a black business owner and I felt it my duty to support him.

Craig set up his business engage enterprise that year, 2006 a business support platform with the magazine of the same name, engage attached to it, as well as 'Flex' for young people and he had invested over £200k into his business.

Unfortunately Engage suffered a loss because his own black people wouldn't support him, and in addition people often tried to solicit his services free instead of paying for his services to help his business grow. It was usually a case of "help me out cuz."

Incidentally many of Craig's business ideas were stolen from him by white people, whom passed off his ideas as their own and thereafter managed to secure funding from large corporate and government bodies where Craig could not.

So you see how important it is that we as black people support each other in business, because if we don't our businesses will ultimately fail and that just sucks for us all.

Incidentally Craig and I are working together on the Economic Programme for the UK, you will hear more about how we are working to unite your nation soon.

We have established that black people actually have money to spend. The USA Government realised that in the 1950s and developed a whole documentary and initiative around how to separate you from your money "How to Sell to the Negro."

The spending power of Britain's black community is now an estimated £300 billion per annum an economic power not to be scoffed at.

In terms of the Capital, London's black-owned businesses generate a combined annual sales turnover of £10bn and employ approximately 100,000 people.

In terms of business, there are currently approximately 16,000 businesses owned by people of black African and Caribbean descent in London alone which makes up 4% of the businesses in London. In addition, 27,000 black Londoners are self-employed.

So if we have money where the hell is evidence of it? We don't own any industry as a collective community which means the money must be going somewhere else. It's going to other communities because we don't buy black enough or as a priority.

At present the black pound doesn't circulate within the black community long enough to make any significant difference, in fact it leaves the moment that it arrives because we don't spend with our own enough to make a significant difference.

The Black community spend 95% of its money outside of our community, and 3% of what we do spend within it, we spend with non-black owned businesses.

The black hair and skin care industry is a perfect example of what you lose by spending outside of your community. Black hair and skin care is a massive money making industry of which we are the main contributors but not the financial beneficiaries.

In the USA, approximately $19 billion is spent annually on hair. In the UK, £5.25 billion is the annual spend, and UK black women account for 80% of total hair product sales.

As the evidence would suggest, the vast majority of people selling products exclusively for black people are not black. A visit to your local beauty supply store, whether in a majority black area or not, will typically reveal the stores are not black-owned and they also contain a slew of brands that are also non-black owned.

I have always been amazed, at how we have allowed other races to infiltrate black hair care to make multimillion pound incomes by opening shops selling your black hair and beauty products to you.

In fact, many of them, like Pak have grown from one shop to massive superstores, all focused on the black woman and her innate passion for spending on her hair and skin.

Other races know that black people like to spend money and you are therefore specifically targeted by them as their consumers.

Asian businesses have the hair care market retail and wholesale sewn up! On lock down! They have a Marcus Garvey style hold on black hair care.

With the control of import of products, they control the distribution, wholesale and retail, working together as a community to open shops and superstores.

Then as one succeeds they open another up the road. Always owned and run by them, employing their own to boost employment and wealth within their own community.

They unite to enhance their economic strength and wealth, but sadly, black communities do not, that is the main reason others can make massive profits from our spending, as we continue to spend with others and not our own.

Buy Black products from Black-Owned Businesses

Asian people are currently the most industrious people on the planet. They are the perfect example of what it takes to build industry through community unity and organisation.

They see a niche, or a gap in the market and they waste no time at all, they jump straight on it, by-passing all the racist systems and just get on with creating business and industry from small businesses in unity with their community.

Jewish, Asian, and White people keep money in their own communities, they buy and sell to each other exclusively in order to increase their wealth. But black people do not seem to share the same collective mind-set when it comes to commerce.

People, we must be conscious of our spending, think big! And bigger! Don't just think about you needing hair care products and go to your nearest and most convenient store which is not black-owned.

Think collective about your community and the impact of your spending. Is it helping the black community? If not then think again and make a conscious effort to spend where your money increases the wealth and well-being of your own.

Not only skin and hair care, but you must support all black-owned businesses from health to clothing, accountants, solicitors, any black-owned business must get your support to help increase the wealth in your community. We must seek them out and give them our support.

As the statistics have shown, other races keep their wealth within their own communities and support each other to build their wealth.

So the cash that you give to companies that sell you your products is not put back into the black community.

Madam CJ Walker

How did Madam CJ Walker become a millionaire business woman? It was through having the custom of her own people.

"I promoted myself into the business of manufacturing hair goods and preparations. I have built my own factory on my own ground. I had to make my own living and my own opportunity. But I made it!" —Madam CJ Walker

She Created specialised hair products for African-American hair, and was one of the first American women to become a self-made millionaire. At a time when women couldn't vote and African American women were legally discriminated against, Madam CJ Walker achieved success against the odds.

Her success surprised the white male business establishment, as she tapped into a huge undeveloped market in black Women's Hair Care, quickly expanding her company across the USA.

This once penniless orphan, was the first American woman to become a self-made millionaire. When she died, she left two-thirds of her fortune to Black charities, and a revolutionary business model for entrepreneurs to follow.

Devin Robinson is a US entrepreneur that specialises in helping the black community take back the haircare industry in the US.

He has an organisation called the Beauty Supply Institute which is an educational institution for aspiring entrepreneurs on how to successfully become Black Beauty Supply Store Owners.

To date Devin Robinson has helped people under the tutelage of his institution open over 80 black-owned beauty supply stores, which has seen the Koren stores in that particular area close down due to black people taking their custom from the Korean owned stores and giving it to the black owned beauty stores. Awesome!

Black Sterling Action Step 6 - Take it Black

It is Time to change the tide people. Take It Black! Take over your hair industry and buy black hair and skin care from black-owned businesses exclusively.

To help you along I have produced a Mobile App Directory aptly named TAKE IT BLACK.

On the Take It Black App you can now find black-owned businesses for hair care products and services from the UK and US. It is FREE android app for consumers and haircare and beauty businesses alike. Go to www.blacksterling.uk for the googleplay link or go to the googleplay store under business/beauty and type in Take It Black.

CHAPTER EIGHT

THE PROVEN PATH TO

COLLECTIVE BLACK WEALTH

"Prepare to operate in an alternative system… A Black Economic System."–Khadijah Ward

Garvey Style

"Negro Producers! Negro Distributers! Negro Consumers! The world of Negros can be self-contained." – Marcus Garvey

My question to you all is, if other races can collectively pool their money and create industry, why can't you? Think about it.

Our brother Malcolm X and others before him such as Marcus Garvey have provided our blue-print to collective black wealth.

Yet fifty plus years after Malcolm's assassination black people across the globe are still demobilised, poor and dependent upon the oppressors system for education and livelihood. That's crazy, Right!

Garvey an orator and staunch proponent of the Black Nationalism and Pan-Africanism movement, created the largest African American organisation, Universal Negro Improvement Association (UNIA) with hundreds of chapters across the world at its height.

At the core of Garvey's vision and programme was Black Economic Self-Reliance. Black people's rights to political self-determination, and the founding of a Black Nation on the continent of Africa.

Over a hundred years ago Garvey united 6 million Black people through the creation of trade and industry. Buying from each other, traded big industries.

"We have to make and manufacture products." He said. He employed over 10,000 Black people in factories, laundries, shops and restaurants. He built buildings all over New York City and the Caribbean.

Garvey provided black people with the blueprint to financial success. He not only told us, but showed us how to control every aspect of the game. "Negro Producers! Negro Distributers! Negro Consumers! The world of Negros can be self-contained." He said.

He built factories, fleet of trucks to distribute the products, he put shops across New York, he built a fleet of commercial steam ships to carry the produce to the caribbean; The Black Star-liner Shipping line. (You may remember the 1975 song by Jamaican reggae recording artist, Fred Locks '7 miles of Black star liner' in tribute to Garvey's steam ships and economic genius.)

The economically independent Black Star Line, an enterprise enabling black people around the Atlantic to exchange goods and services, was a symbol of pride for black people which attracted more members to the UNIA.

The company's three ships were owned and operated by black people and made travel and trade possible between the United States, Caribbean, Central American, and African stops.

Each ship costing $2000 dollars at that time, equates to approximately quarter of a £million in today's currency.

The shipping line facilitated the transportation of goods and intended eventually transport African Americans throughout the African global economy.

It was one among many businesses which the UNIA originated, such as the Universal Printing House, Negro Factories Corporation, and the widely distributed and highly successful Negro World weekly newspaper.

All of the above are demonstrative of his blue-print to the proven path to collective black wealth right there.

Malcolm X on the other hand, through the Nation of Islam, created economic control, building up Black communities with industry, stores and mosques driving out drug dealers and criminals.

Today the Nation of Islam owns hundreds of businesses nationwide and operates its own farm to support its members.

From the founder of the Nation of Islam's, Elijah Muhammed's economic blue-print, Malcolm X created economic control, building up black communities with industry, stores and mosques driving out drug dealers and criminals.

Today the Nation of Islam owns hundreds of businesses nationwide and operates its own farms to support its members.

*"The Black man has to be reeducated to the importance of supporting Black business, but the Black man himself has to be made aware of the importance of going into business. Once you and I go into business we own and operate at least the businesses in our own community. We will be developing a situation wherein we will be able to create employment for the people in the community. Once we create employment it will eliminate the necessity of having to act ignorantly and disgracefully boycotting some c*****r some place else trying to beg him for a job...Anytime you have to rely upon your enemy for a job you are in bad shape" —Malcolm X*

"The economic philosophy of Black Nationalism only means that we have to become involved in a program of reeducation to educate our people into the importance of knowing that when you spend your dollar out of the community in which you live, the community in which you spend your money becomes richer and richer; the community out which you take your money becomes poorer and poorer."—Malcolm X

The US Economic Bus Movement

We all know and love Martin Luther King. However, before Martin Luther became 'conscious' that is to say he awoke to the real problems of black people integrating within white people's systems, he was used by the US Government Kennedy's Administration to stop the real black freedom movement which was economical.

The 1955 bus boycott which lasted for a year, came about from the Jim Crow racial segregation laws which in practice meant that black people were not hired as bus drivers, they were only allowed to ride on the back of the bus and had to surrender their seats to white people if required them.

Remember in the preface we spoke about the difference between segregation and separation. Segregation is bad for us and separation is good.

To refresh your memory, segregation is not good for black people, because it means even though we may be all together in a black area we are not in control of the infrastructures or our lives. In fact we are under control of the white power structure and systems.

Economical development and empowerment was occurring in the black neighbourhoods through the bus boycotts. Black people were running their own bus lines and stopped riding the white bus.

The boycotters organised a system of carpooling. People with cars also volunteered to take people to wherever they wanted to travel. In support of the boycott black owners of taxies charged customers the same price as a bus ticket.

Black people also walked to work in the city, not only did they refuse to ride the white buses they also would not buy anything in the city from the white businesses. They brought their lunches in sacks from home.

The black community stopped paying out money to white businesses , they united and kept the money inside of their own community.

The boycotts were extremely effective it brought the white economic system in many cities across the United States to their knees. Black people were economically destroying cities.

The white American power structure felt that they had to put a stop to the bus boycott, they did not want black people being economically independent, the situation was not good for white economics. So President Kennedy called all black leaders to Washington to tell them, and I quote " stop this 'Negronomics' change the focus to voter registration and civil rights." Enter Martin Luther.

Kennedy knew exactly what he was doing when he requested a focus change to voter registration and civil rights. These areas are under the control of the white American system. There is no self-reliant economical outcome for the black nation in either of those two subjects, they are solutions for integration.

Cast your mind back to a section of this book ' The Secret of selling to the Negro" White people use the black community as their commodities and they will do everything possible to keep it that way. Black money, your money is required to feed the system.

In 1956 the bus segregation laws were found to be unconstitutional which meant that now black people were authorised to sit anywhere that they wanted.

In my opinion the white power structure won, integration within the white systems was achieved. Yes, we can sit where we want but we are not in control of the buses, we do not own the bus, we are economically dependent upon their system. The system allowed black people. The systems laws and allowances enabled integration, they gave it to you. Integration makes black people lazy and the power structure knows that. If they allow us to integrate we will not strive for economic self-reliance

Black Wall Street

Remember Black Wall Street, the most prosperous black community of 1921 in the US. The city of Greenwood, Oklahoma, well Greenwood, became the most economically prosperous black community in the history of the United States. Black Wall Street was created through unity, organisation and self-reliance of black communities.

As of 1921, the Black-owned town had 15 grocery stores, two movie theatres, four drug stores, two public schools, four barbecue/chilli parlours, and 13 churches. All of this was created and run by black people. The town was the wealthiest Black community in the United States, more prosperous than the white-run community next door. In fact black wall street used to provide financial assistance, loans to neighbouring white communities. This thriving black community soon led to a great deal of animosity.

A large-scale, racially motivated conflict occurred in which a group of whites attacked the black community of Tulsa, Oklahoma which resulted in the Greenwood District, 'the Black Wall Street' the wealthiest black community in the United States, being burned to the ground, most likely by the Klu Klux Klan.

Do not be discouraged or phased by Black Wall Street being burnt down, by white supremacists. If we do not try again and come back bigger and better then they would have won.

Black Wall Street is significant because it shows black people can be in control of themselves and organised, operating in unity to achieve economic wealth post-slavery. We done it once we can do it again.

Come Back Bigger and Better!

If other races collectively pool their money together and create industry, why can't you?

There is overwhelming evidence that the black community does not spend with its own enough to make a significant difference in terms of building industry, institutions and creating collective wealth.

Remember, we live in a capitalist society, so wealth as a collective unit is the key to power and control. As discussed the white community is a perfect example of collective wealth in operation and their systems speak for themselves.

White people can build and achieve wealth as a community through this white infrastructure simply because the euro-centric system is built to benefit them. And our infrastructures should be built to benefit us.

Black people as a collective unit can live as a wealthy and productive community, there is no need to strive to integrate and live off what little crumbs are thrown to us through this system.

You and I together can achieve a high standard of living outside of this current system through the creation of our own systems, that you are in control of. Remember, self-reliance is economic control.

We must be loyal to each other, and those of us that manage to become wealthy should not run to escape the ghetto and live as wealthy individuals in white communities. You must work in unity with other black people to create the same type of communities for the rest of your brothers and sisters.

The masses cannot be left to remain trapped and suffering in the ghetto while we live it up in a Kensington & Chelsea lifestyle, it should not be a case of 'I'm all right jack.' We are all in this together.

Take a Leaf From Other Communities

Other communities have achieved independent success and so can the black community. As a so called 'minority' community it is possible to co-exist with other communities but still be in control of your own.

If you want to get a glimpse of economic power of a minority group, take a look at both the Asian and Irish community.

In a word, Bollywood! The Asian-owned Bollywood is classified as the biggest movie industry in the world in terms of the amount of people employed and number of films produced.

Bollywood was mirrored on Hollywood, they did not beg for a piece of Hollywood's action, they got their own, goddammit! (I like saying goddammit - Hahaha.)

The UK civil engineering and construction industry are massive industries. I use them as an example as I have worked in both and I have seen them operate from the inside.

There is no question that the Irish have the construction industry on lock down! They own it.

Incidentally, I worked for a family run construction company, and they were some Racist Mother Fxxkers! No names mentioned, they know who they are.

I was Tuped over to their corporate plantation (Transfer of undertakings. Its effect is to move employees and any liabilities associated with them from the old employer to the new employer by operation of law), from a senior management position earning 70k plus a 20% annual bonus. I got too comfortable on their plantation and I suffered the consequences. Make no mistake you are under their control and they can do with you what they will anytime they feel like it. So, there was no way on gods green earth they were going to allow me to continue earning big bucks from them, so they drove me out the door within three months by undermining my position.

First they made me report to an uneducated old hag of a munchkin and when I fought that and it didn't make me leave they made me redundant.

Sorry, I digressed for a moment, I just wanted to give you another example of how they are the controllers of the system, as it is their system.

So if you work on their corporate plantation they have the power to kick you out the door whenever they like. And when you are black it will be more often than not. So the best thing to do is not to work for the racist Mother Fxxkers in the first place.

Anyway as a business owner I joined an Irish construction network just to see just exactly how they operate with a view to mirroring something similar. I have seen these networks in action, all different business sectors and industries, Irish-owned, working together, they are effective, they work!

They create business and job opportunities for each other from all sectors not just construction, it included, law, accountancy, printing, you name it. And that is how they keep the money circulating within their own community to build industry and wealth.

Yes, they let me inside of their network but I was the only black person at the networking events. On one occasion I took my friend Craig Cordice with me so there were two token black people in the room.

I was welcomed at the networks, nonetheless people were surprised to see me there. In fact one of the members asked me what my Irish connection was? Clearly it was odd that a black woman would be at an Irish event. I replied, my "grandfather was Irish"... *Hahahahahaha.*

Anyhow, construction equals housing and buildings, highly important, but who runs it? It's The Irish. Yes, they are a white community and they were not enslaved for 400 years, nor is the racism that they experienced to-date as deep or as comparable as the black community, but this system puts people at different levels, including their own. And Irish people were at the bottom of the white ladder, to the point where the English tried to wipe them out. That is all I am saying about that as this is not a book on Irish history.

You may remember prior to the induction of the Race Relations Act 1975, the 'No Blacks, No Irish, No Dogs' signs back in the 1960s which were displayed in the windows of private landlords. It was common place and deemed as normal and acceptable behaviour.

Many Irish business people in their discussions of experiences of racism in Britain have told of their exclusion in gaining access to housing, being refused employment and bank loans for businesses.

So they pooled together their pounds and pence and they overcame their discrimination by uniting and organising. Collectively pooling their money, setting up networks and businesses, buying and selling their products and services to each other, employing each other and building housing and industry and institutions.

They have experienced their own type of racism by the system and have risen above it, and in that regard they may be used as an example of collective working.

As a community, we, black people have the capacity to build our own economic system, what we need now is the heart to unite and gain control of the economy in our own communities. Then we will not have to Pickett, boycott or beg for equality and inclusion from the controllers of the euro-centric system.

CHAPTER NINE

BLACK STERLING - THE FINAL CHAPTER

"Your current situation is not your final destination "

– *Khadijah Ward*

Do You Really Understand Money?

"Your love gives me such a thrill, but your love don't pay my bills...I need Money! Whole lotta moneeeey..." – *60s Singer-Songwriter Barrett Strong*

Let me tell you a quick story... In the 80s and 90s I lived three minutes away from The Royal Mint. The limited company that is wholly owned by Her Majesty's Treasury that produces coins for the United Kingdom, operating under the name Royal Mint Ltd. The first pound coin did not manifest until 1489, under Henry VII, which was called a sovereign. (The explanation of Royal Mint is for my US brothers and sisters that may be reading this book.)

I used to look at that vast Royal Mint building everyday, feel the presence of the money and dream of how I could get a taste of some of it. I didn't really understand the banking system or money, all I knew, was that I wanted it.

Like you, I too was a product of the system that dictated that I must obtain money in order to live my life. Either that or not be part of the monetary system and live rough on the streets. One had a choice, although the choice was extremely one-sided weighing heavily toward the side of working inside the system.

In my early years I paid for everything in cash as I was told by my parents to save my money and always pay for goods in cash. That way you do not owe anybody anything. And that was the beginning and end of my lessons in financial banking from my parents.

However on my life journey I learned that saving money didn't particularly equal wealth, and I was on a quest for wealth! Although I had no idea how I was going to get there.

Saving, with the bank hardly a wealth building platform it would seem. In fact, in today's economy, depending on the type of bank account that one has you may receive one to five percent interest on your money or three percent annually. And in addition should the cost of living increase by ten percent for example you may lose money on your savings. Saving your money in this current banking system is beneficial only to the institution of the bank.

In my teens I had a building society account, but in the 80s I visited my local bank to open a bank account. Those were the days when one could get an actual meeting with the bank manager, in fact they encouraged it.

Played by the Bank Manager

The bank manager wasn't much older than I, he began engaging in conversation asking me if I knew who the actor Brad Pitt was. He was surprised that I didn't as his wife and all the ladies were besotted with this US actor, he said.

The Bank manager also informed me that he met his wife at the bank, and now they were an item they had to work in separate locations due to banking policy etcetera, etcetera. Clearly I did not need to know that but it seems he was warming me up for the big sale.

He was talking a lot and went on to inform me of how the banking system worked. We need your money, he said with a charming smile. He went on to say, you leave your money in the bank and we gamble with it every day on the stock exchange throughout the night, but we always have enough to put it back giving the customer access to their money should they need it. That's the day I found out that bankers were a bunch of gamblers, elite bookies.

Anyhow, the bank manager played me using the 'bait and trap' system to get me into credit card borrowing, as he literally threw the credit card form at me told me to sign, 'there and there' and I fell for it. The Access credit card it was called then.

I completely ignored my parents advice about paying in cash, I accepted the card and went on a shopping spree racking up £4000 worth of debt on restaurants, clothes and pretty shoes.

When the bill arrived, I could not believe my eyes. However I was happy to see that there was a minimum payment of £5 per month. That happiness turned to dismay when I worked out that I would be paying this debt back until I reached retirement age. And, the vast amount of money in interest the bank would accumulate was astounding.

I went to see my bank manager about the debt, and he convinced (note the first three letters of the word Con-vince) me to take out a loan to pay off the credit card as the loan had a lower interest rate. I ended up in £20k worth of debt in my early twenties. And that brothers and sisters is the win-win system of and for the bank. I won't tell you how I got out of the debt as that remains a conversation for off the record.

Clearly the use of the credit cards helps the bank earn substantial amounts of money from you and I. And today where we pay for everything using the debit card it allows the bank to hold onto our money even longer and gamble with impunity, making obscene amounts of money for themselves in the process. You cannot withdraw £5 from the cashpoint but you can pay for £5 worth of goods using your debit card - This procedure enables the bank to hold onto your money longer and use it at will. Are you getting this?

Think about it, you need a bank account for everything. Even people claiming £70 per week job seekers allowance have to have a bank account. The system is set up in such a way that it has a hold on your money which ever way you turn, and you will find it very hard to function without the use of a bank account.

Later on in life I learnt to invest my money in property and gold which provide good returns. Nine carat gold is not a good investment as it only consists of a fraction of gold. Whereby twenty-four carat gold is pure gold. Eighteen carat is 75% gold and twenty-two carat is I believe is about 78%.

Small gold bullion bars are also a good investment which can be purchased directly from the Royal Mint. Gold holds its value and you can carry it with you, if for instance you needed to flee or leave the country you could trade it where ever you go. Remember, gold is accepted world-wide.

Whereby with sterling, the pound, you are unlikely to receive the full value due to currency devaluations, negative interest rates, and minimal economic growth.

In addition if there is a banking crash, that's it! You will be denied access to your own money it's gone! Remember the crash of 1921 People were banging on the doors of banks for their money to no avail. People even committed suicide due to losing life savings.

And the financial crisis of 2008, a result of bankers playing fast and loose with your money and getting it wrong. We the UK taxpayer had to bail out the banks and we are still paying the price today on its tenth anniversary.

A Bank Boss's Booboo

Around 2003 it made front page news that the boss of Britain's biggest credit card company astonished the public with what appeared to be a vote of no confidence in his own product, the credit card.

The £1.7m-a-year chief executive of Barclays, which owns Barclaycard, admitted he did not use his or anyone else's plastic to borrow money "because it's too expensive". He also revealed urging his children not to rack up debts on their cards either.

His confession came after he was accused of using marketing tactics that amounted to "a bait and a trap" to get people into "a position of chronic borrowing" and inevitable debt. The very 'bait and trap' used on me by my bank manager.

After falling for the trappings of loans and debt I learnt that credit cards keep you a slave to the system on a conveyor belt of paying back leaving you with empty pockets.

And saving money doesn't really give you any real return on your money. Banks benefit from customers saving their money, however you as a customer do not. Remember the bank uses your money to gamble and make more money for itself using the promise of interest return as an illusion that you will make money when in fact it is so minimal it is of no real benefit to you at all.

Be warned, credit cards are a complete rip off! They are traps for the poor and should not be used unless you can afford to pay off every transaction in cash within the 21 or 30 days that they give you to clear the debt without incurring interest.

Sterling

This final chapter helps you to understand money and aims to show you how your money can work for you as an individual.

In that collectively we can become Sovereign with independent power, and in so doing, create our own over-arching legal system of banking, control our own infrastructures and economic systems.

Use of the word "sterling" did not arise until after the Norman Conquest, and it originally referred to pennies not pounds.

The Anglo-Saxon King Offa is credited with introducing the system of money to central and southern England in the latter half of the eighth Century, overseeing the minting of the earliest English silver pennies emblazoned with his name.

The pound was a unit of account in Anglo-Saxon England, equal to 240 silver pennies and equivalent to one pound weight of silver. It evolved into the modern British currency, the pound sterling.

Is Money Everything Or The Only Thing?

Money isn't everything, or is it? The lyrics of Barrett Strong's song seem to suggest that it is.

Nonetheless, there remains a prevalent misconception regarding money as to its importance. Some consider it as unimportant and some may profess to not even care about it . However, the fact that one cannot obtain groceries, buy a car, a house or cater to ones basic human needs without money, demonstrates that it is somewhat of high importance to the human existence in the modern world.

As does the assertion by certain 'gang members' on the streets of London that claim they can earn up to a £1000 per day on the street as opposed to £10 an hour working for the likes of Burger King.

And therefore, are willing to use the streets as their family, criminal activities as career prospects and the risk of death as the ultimate disciplinary action, all for the sake of money. These actions I believe are brought about by a combination of the ignorance of self and that of money. If our young had knowledge and love of self coupled with financial expertise we would be seeing community spirit, young business owners and collaborative nation building as opposed to the current street situation. But that's on us as adults which is covered throughout the chapters of this book.

I am unaware whether you as an individual reading this book have an abundance of money or not, but undoubtedly, if you are living on planet earth, money is the influencing and determining factor in how you live your life.

If you do have money, take a moment and think about how your life would change with the sudden loss of your money. I am sure the images that you conjure up do not make you feel good at all.

For those of you that do not have so much money, take a moment and really imagine your ideal lifestyle if you had an abundance of money…Feels great right!

Our feelings surrounding money, whether we believe it to be important or not are a result of the systems that we live under. Having being introduced to money as the central and controlling component to every facet of our lives - The system of banking.

You see the problem is, we as individual African-Caribbean people and as a nation, simply do not understand money, investment or the banking system well enough to make it work for us.

So at present our lack of financial knowledge leads to our current state, in that we are perishing, we are infrastructure deficient and economically disconnected. We do not invest in ourselves as individuals or collectively in each other as a nation.

The Power of the Banking System

Those that control the banking system control the people. Via the banking system the 'elite' one percent dictate our behaviour and weld power over the people's actions in our pursuit of happiness, that we have been made to believe can only be obtained through the access of money.

But what is money really? It isn't a precious resource like gold. It is simply paper that has been accorded the seal of approval of a high standing value system. Namely, the Bank of England, the UK power structure and controller of the monetary system.

Have you ever thought about the huge infrastructure behind the money? The Bank of England, which created this powerful 'promise to pay' legal system with paper at the helm.

England's naval defeat by France in the 1690 Battle of Beachy Head led to King William III establishing the Bank of England to fund his continued war with France. The bank began issuing notes in 1695 with the promise to pay the bearer the value of the note on demand.

The Bank of England was the first bank to initiate the permanent issue of banknotes. Banknotes began to circulate in England soon after the establishment of the Bank of England. They were initially hand-written. Banknotes are generally legal tender, meaning that medium of payment is allowed by law or recognised by a legal system to be valid for meeting a financial obligation.

Paper money is essentially a promise to pay. Take a note from your wallet and read it, you will find that is what it will say. A promissory clause printed on the bank note to give the bearer means the weight in sterling silver. Which makes the banknote legal tender for that amount. The obligation on the part of the Bank is to exchange a banknote for sterling silver of an equivalent amount.

Historically, banks sought to ensure that they could always pay customers in coins when they presented banknotes for payment. A practice of backing notes with something of substance. Legally you should be able to take your bank notes to the bank of England in exchange for silver.

However, today there are so many notes in circulation that the Banks do not have enough gold or silver to operate that system so the money we hold doesn't really have any value.

Learn the Money Game

The point of providing you with this information is to simply say we as a black nation, a collective, can set up our own monetary systems of banking, just as the Bank of England did, but as a less 'cut throat' system. Ours should work in favour of the people.

As a community, we may benefit from introducing a banking system that does not apply interest. A non-rip off banking system sounds very appealing does it not? Once we control our own banking institution we can then build up the infrastructures to create our own independent political party, as gaining political power takes money and sound infrastructures. Imagine, no more voting for those that clearly do not have our best interests at heart.

We have plenty of money as a nation, so when are we going to decide that nation building is just as important as the other things that we spend our money on, such as entertainment, the short-term 'feel good' factor.

A complete paradigm shift is required to become infrastructure efficient economically connected between the money we have and how to invest it.

Learning to play a sophisticated role in the money game and in-turn become politically savvy as individuals and a nation is absolutely paramount for the survival of our nation. And as individuals we should understand finance and learn how to invest in business to get good returns on our money for future growth and prosperity.

Donating to our own 'good cause' organisations instead of the likes of some of the well known charities that really do not benefit our young or our people in general will enhance our strength as a nation.

And, instead of just going to the pictures and watching films such as Black Panther, we could have seen further than then film itself as an investment opportunity and purchased Marvel/Disney stocks. I say this because Disney made billions from the movie (our money), therefore anyone with shares in the company would have made a nice little earner too.

Disney and the likes are white-owned companies, however that is just an example of how if you must give your money away in that direction try your utmost to get a return on your investment.

Crypto currencies are becoming a big thing now for investments. I personally haven't invested as yet, however there is a US based black-owned crypto company called Storji you can check it out to see if it is suitable to meet your needs. And you may want to invest in a recommended trustworthy financial advisor prior to any investment ventures.

Investing money in companies is a valid investment vehicle, risky, but it can also yield high returns. Investing in charities by donation as an individual or via taxes if you are a business. These are investments where the return will be evidenced within your community.

Disclaimer: Always seek financial advice before venturing into any financial investments.

It is essential to create community networks, reintroduce the system of bartering to aid businesses that are strapped for cash. As well as donate, contribute and invest money to each others causes.

Collecting small amounts of money can add up to huge sums. Eventually, with our own banking system, community networks and infrastructures will enable us to build our own independent political party, and in-turn assert our power as a collective force to be reckoned with by this European financial and political arena.

As a nation you must remain alert to the real issues behind the systems, which is economics, political power and wealth. These are the things that we need to create for ourselves.

Together we will become competitors instead of the oppressed and build our black economic infrastructure and systems for your community. We will create, share, and multiply wealth.

The Black Sterling Charity Group '2nd2None' wants to begin working with communities across the UK to create a level playing field for black people as a collective group of people to become competitors in the economic market.

Our aim is to build a Black Economic infrastructures over time that encompasses all of the areas of industry and institutions that are covered within this book. We plan to do this by teaming up with other organisations throughout the UK.

What we want to achieve with you and for you will be developed in phases, and over time we will also work with our brothers and sisters across the globe to increase our economic strength.

Well, beautiful Black people, I hope that you enjoyed reading the book Black Sterling. Please ask all of your family and friends to buy it for their own enlightenment and put this book in the hands of you children. 50% of the proceeds of total book sales of Black Sterling will be directed toward The Black Sterling Charity to kickstart funding for your Black Economic Systems.

Remember, you have been accorded a natural great honour, and that honour, is being born African (Black). With that honour comes great responsibility, but also challenges, challenges that can be overcome to achieve great things when you rise and unite.

Be conscious of your rich and powerful heritage, imagine, and be inspired by your ancestors to do bigger and better for yourself and for us all.

Strive to become authors, creators, entrepreneurs, business owners and developers of industry. Above all love, and support your brothers and sisters in business by donating, buying and selling from your own to build collective wealth and industry.

Your current situation is not your final destination – Khadijah Ward

Black Sterling Action Step 7

This is the final step that you can take towards investing in the economic future for you and your community. It is divided into sub-steps from A-I.

A. Review all of the previous actions steps.

B. Turn your paper money into an asset. Use it to invest in small gold bullion or 18/22/24 carat pieces.

C. With people you can trust group together form a co-op and purchase property that you can use to rent out.

D. If you can, avoid using credit cards to minimise the accumulation of debt and paying interest to the banks.

E. Teach your children the art of finance and investment.

F. Buy Black! Support your brothers and sisters to take back the hair care industry. Download the 'Take it Black' Mobile App directory of the black-owned haircare and beauty stores across the UK on google stores. https://play.google.com/store/apps/details?id=com.app.takeitblack

G. Register your email address to be notified of the launch of phase one with further details and updates of your Economic Programme and a part of your great future. www.blacksterling.uk

H. See the bigger picture, help us to help you build social developments, finance causes to build institutions, infrastructures and political power in your community. Donate £1 per week to the Nexus black business project. https://www.gofundme.com/nexusforblackbusiness

I. If you are a business owner donate to some of our charitable organisations that work with young people such as: www.manhoodacademy.co.uk and www.accessuk.org

Brothers and sisters, we were an independent (African) black nation in the past. It was our way of life before the rude interruption of the Europeans. We have done it before and we can do it again.

Remember our heritage is that of Kings, Queens and Riches, we are decedents of the richest man that ever lived, Mansa Musa. Also remember our Superhero Marcus Garvey the economic genius that gave us the powerful blueprint to economic self-reliance and independence.

"Negro Producers! Negro Distributers! Negro Consumers! The world of Negros can be self-contained." '-Marcus Garvey

Prepare to operate in an alternative system… A Black Economic System – Khadijah Ward

ABOUT THE AUTHOR

Khadijah Ward is an Author, Public Speaker, Social Critic, escapee of the plantation economy and an avid promoter of Black Economic Self-Reliance and empowerment of people.
She is also a Mother of two, and grandmother of five.
Watch out for her forthcoming book…
Dark Girl Boss…From Self-Hate to Great.

Printed in Great Britain
by Amazon